POWER HOUSE

**Turbo boost your effectiveness
and start making a serious impact**

MIKE CLAYTON

CAPSTONE
A Wiley Brand

This edition first published 2015

© 2015 Mike Clayton

Registered office
John Wiley and Sons Ltd, The Atrium, Southern Gate, Chichester, West Sussex,
PO19 8SQ, United Kingdom

For details of our global editorial offices, for customer services and for information about how to apply for permission to reuse the copyright material in this book please see our website at www.wiley.com.

Wiley publishes in a variety of print and electronic formats and by print-on-demand. Some material included with standard print versions of this book may not be included in e-books or in print-on-demand. If this book refers to media such as a CD or DVD that is not included in the version you purchased, you may download this material at http://booksupport.wiley.com. For more information about Wiley products, visit www.wiley.com.

Designations used by companies to distinguish their products are often claimed as trademarks. All brand names and product names used in this book and on its cover are trade names, service marks, trademark or registered trademarks of their respective owners. The publisher and the book are not associated with any product or vendor mentioned in this book. None of the companies referenced within the book have endorsed the book.

Cataloging-in-Publication Data for this book is available from the Library of Congress.

A catalogue record for this book is available from the British Library.

ISBN 978-0-857-08556-6 (paperback)
ISBN 978-0-857-08558-0 (ebk)   ISBN 978-0-857-08557-3 (ebk)

Cover Design: Wiley
Cover Images: @Shutterstock.com/maxuser

Set in 10/14.5pt in Palatino LT Std by Laserwords Private Limited, Chennai, India.
Printed in Great Britain by TJ International Ltd, Padstow, Cornwall, UK

Powerhouse *(noun): somebody who is full of energy, highly effective, and therefore very productive.*

CONTENTS

INTRODUCTION

*Powerhouse (noun): somebody who is full of energy,
highly effective, and therefore very productive.*

There is so much you want to get done in a day and modern life is making ever more demands. Adding to your desire for a successful career, a fulfilled private life and some form of lifetime achievement you can be proud of are all of the pressures of living and interacting socially.

Yet the one thing modern technology has not given us – and will almost certainly never provide – is more time. So the answer must be ever greater levels of productivity.

Is it any surprise therefore that many people's bookshelves are groaning with productivity and time saving manuals, and that bloggers and coaches are offering a constant stream of tips and advice? Oh no! More things to add to your reading list.

Time management and greater productivity are not the answer. The answer is not about how much you can do, but what you do and how you do it. If you choose the right things to do, and you do them in the right way, you will be productive. But not just 'lots of stuff done-productive': you will be 'effective-productive'.

The difference is essential: getting lots of stuff done means nothing unless the stuff you do matters. That is what effectiveness is about: about doing what matters; what will make a difference that counts.

What Does it Mean to Be a 'Powerhouse'?

Effective action defines Powerhouse. But one thing that you won't find in this book is a single definition of what being a Powerhouse means. It means far more than one thing and goes beyond the normal day-to-day meaning of effectiveness:

> **effective** (adjective): causing the desired result, successful, able to deliver what matters.

It is a mentality and approach that delivers outstanding productivity and exceptional outcomes, and makes a vivid, lasting, and positive impression on the people around you.

Becoming a Powerhouse means:

- Choosing to do the right things.
- Doing the right things for the right reasons.
- Doing the right things right.
- Working with the people around you.
- Getting the best from the people around you.
- Getting the best from yourself.
- Being prepared for the unexpected.
- Handling the unexpected.
- Knowing when and how to stop.
- Extending your Powerhouse capabilities to your whole organization.

These definitions form the agenda for this book. Over the next ten chapters, you will learn how to bring full effectiveness to everything you do. Each chapter will also show you how to turn up one of ten Power Switches, to transform yourself – and your organization – into a Powerhouse.

Chapter 1: **Self-Control: Choose to Do the Right Things**

The first step is to identify and evaluate all of your opportunities. Then, decide which ones to pursue. Let these become your compelling causes, and focus almost exclusively on them. This is about self-control.

Master Switch: Self-Control

Chapter 2: **Judgement: Do the Right Things for the Right Reasons**

You need to be clear why you are pursuing each of your compelling causes, for two reasons – personal and organizational. The organizational reason is that you will almost certainly be accountable for how you will be using your time and spending your resources, and the personal reason is that we all need to know the answer to the question 'why?' Without a reason, there is no motivation. We'll cover how to justify your choices and learn about judgement.

Power Switch: Judgement

Chapter 3: **Productivity: Do the Right Things Right**

Now is the time to think about how you are going to accomplish what you set out to do. This is about productivity and Chapter 3 splits this into four stages: planning, preparing, performing and postparing. Don't worry if you haven't heard the word 'postparing' – neither had I before I started work on this book.

Power Switch: Productivity

Chapter 4: Relationships: Work With the People Around You

You need to be able to enlist the support of the people around you: colleagues, team-members, bosses, suppliers and customers. Their active support will be a big factor in your success. And it is not just dealing with opposition that is important; it is positive support. So we will look at how you can build support for your work in Chapter 4. This is about relationships.

Power Switch: Relationships

Chapter 5: Leadership: Get the Best From the People Around You

More than support, you may also need active help. Decide which people with what skills you will need, engage their help, and give them the leadership that will get the best from them. This will be our agenda for Chapter 5.

Power Switch: Leadership

Chapter 6: Conduct: Get the Best From Yourself

The ways that you think and act will determine how effective you are in your choices, your productivity and in the way people regard you. This is all about your conduct.

Power Switch: Conduct

Chapter 7: Perception: Be Prepared for the Unexpected

Shift happens: are you able to anticipate it by reading people, seeing around corners and spotting risks? This is a matter of your perception.

Power Switch: Perception

Chapter 8:   Resilience: Handle the Unexpected

> Whether you spotted it or not, when shift happens, how will you respond to events? If you can keep going in the face of adversity, dealing with the challenges you encounter and keeping a feeling of calm and control, that's resilience.
>
> Power Switch: Resilience

Chapter 9:   Growth: Know When and Where to Stop

> Of course, you need to know when to stop, but you must also know where to stop, so that your Powerhouse performance is a springboard for your next compelling cause. This demands the ability to grow with each experience.
>
> Power Switch: Growth

In the final chapter, I will show you how to extend your Powerhouse capabilities to help the whole of your organization to become a Powerhouse Organization.

Chapter 10: Culture: Create a Powerhouse Organization

> Can you take what you have learned and start to transform the whole organization around you? Wouldn't that be great? If you want to apply the Powerhouse principles strategically, to create a true Powerhouse culture, Chapter 10 will give you the places to start.
>
> Organizational Power Switch: Culture

Each switch represents a capability that you can increase with learning and practice. As you turn all of the switches up to maximum, you will become a Powerhouse.

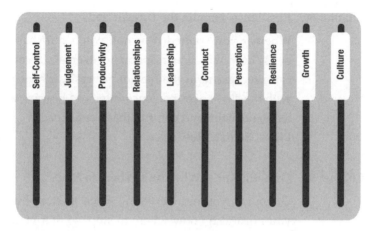

Ten switch console

What You Need to Become a Powerhouse

Becoming a Powerhouse requires a combination of mental attitude and a practical approach that balances different perspectives, focuses ruthlessly, yet remains adaptable in the face of changing circumstances. This requires a combination of efficiency, rigour and a survival edge. This is worthwhile, but not easy. Two things will help:

1. doing the right thing for you, and
2. being fit for Powerhouse performance.

1. Doing the Right Thing for You

Being a Powerhouse will come to you far more easily when you enjoy what you are doing, and are doing something you are good at. You choose the work that brings you joy, and the key lies at the intersection of:

- The things you love to do.
- The things you are good at.
- The things you like best about work.

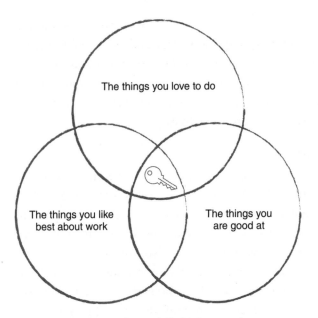

The key to the work that brings you joy

One of the main reasons we fail to achieve what we set out to do is not being clear enough about exactly what the outcome will look like if we do the right things. Always start by asking yourself: 'what will success look like?' So your first step is to define what you want to achieve with clarity and precision, defining success and being clear what it is for.

- What is most important about your job?
- Who does your work serve?
- What is your job really about?
- What do you want to achieve?
- What is your answer to 'why'?

2. Get Fit for Powerhouse Performance

Fitter, healthier people perform better. Don't think that you can swallow this book whole and get instant results. You need to invest time, energy and perseverance. You also need to be fit for a Powerhouse lifestyle, investing in good rest, regular exercise and excellent nutrition.

Powerhouse performance rests on willpower. Modern research shows that this requires energy and as we go through the day willpower depletes, just as the batteries in your phone deplete. So to avoid your brain becoming mushy and your physical strength draining away, it is essential to make re-charging your energy levels a critical activity.

Good Rest

It is not just enough to go home at the end of the day. Make rest and relaxation a priority. Allow time for socializing, for laughing, for relaxing and, vitally, for sleep. Many people with a Powerhouse mind-set will find it hard to switch off at the end of the day. So take your sleep seriously: not by worrying about it, but by setting up the conditions for good sleep. Gradually wind down towards the end of your waking day, dim the lights, engage in more relaxing activities and refrain from stimulant drugs like caffeine (which makes sleeping more difficult) and alcohol (which may make you sleepy, but disrupts your sleep). Have your bed in a cool room with fresh air and, if necessary, write down anything that is on your mind before turning out the light.

Regular Exercise

A regular, moderate exercise regime will increase your resilience and give you a greater capacity for physical and mental effort. You may feel it will take up time in your day, but the amount of effective and productive time it will give you back makes short bouts of exercise an excellent investment. It is no coincidence that most of businesses' most successful and most effective people make time for half an hour of exercise during each working day.

Excellent Nutrition

A rushed meal of junk food at your desk is the cliché of modern office life. On the other hand, I hope I have already made the case for fresh air, exercise and a break – possibly some social-izing. If you are going to work effectively and exercise too, your body will need good fuel to power it. Choose your food wisely and have things like nuts and fruit as your regular snacks.

Additional Resources

Powerhouse is a freestanding book with everything you need to become ... a Powerhouse. But if you want a few extras, like templates for some of the tools, and maybe a few videos with key ideas, then take a look at the Powerhouse website, at www.beapowerhouse.co.uk.

1
Self-Control
Choose to Do the Right Things

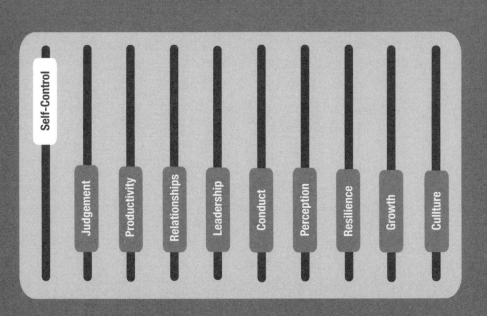

Self-Control

Judgement

Productivity

Relationships

Leadership

Conduct

Perception

Resilience

Growth

Culture

The problem is busyness without doing the business; of getting to the end of the day having done lots and achieved nothing. It's easy to do and often happens when you become seduced by easy, absorbing, but unimportant tasks. To become a *Powerhouse*, you must refine your clarity of purpose to focus your energy on what matters. This means choosing the right things to do and having the self-control to set other things aside.

When I was a student, we would often drive into the Devon countryside, looking for a pub to spend a pleasant afternoon in. It was on one of the very last of these outings, shortly before my friends and I were due to graduate and start our working lives, that we took a turn between two high hedges and found ourselves on an un-made road – little more than a farm track. As we drove along it, the surface got worse, and then we saw a hand-painted sign, doubtless put up by a local farmer. The sign read:

> *'Choose your rut carefully – you're going to be in it for a long time.'*

Focused Busyness

Focused busyness means doing stuff that really makes a difference.

What a perfect warning about adult life: forced either to carry on the way you are going or hit reverse and go backwards. No option to jump out of the rut and choose a new direction. And many of us live lives a little like that, getting to the end of each day, having done lots … and achieved nothing.

I call this 'busyness without doing the business'.

Busyness Without Doing the Business

The consequence of this constantly busy lifestyle is rarely any great sense of success or fulfilment. It often doesn't even produce much in the way of results. All it has to offer is exhaustion.

So, many of us respond by working harder, by becoming more competent and by taking on more responsibility. The 'one more push' approach to happiness. The problem is that the one more push is often in the wrong direction; often a push further along your existing rut. Competence, doing your job and trying harder are not enough.

The best you will do is to consolidate your existing position in your rut, moving up one small step at a time when circumstances permit. Who wants to consolidate a position where you are forever busy and never truly successful?

What is the solution? The solution is 'focused busyness'.

Focused busyness means doing stuff that really makes a difference.

Becoming a Powerhouse means choosing the right things to do and having the self-control to set other things aside.

Powerhouse Effectiveness and Rules

If you learn the rules and work within them, you are always going to be more effective than if you are constantly fighting against them. Changing the rules is hard and so, if you set out to do this, be sure it really matters and is the right thing to do. Wantonly fighting the rules or trying to cheat the system is not noble or wise.

Sometimes, however, it does make sense to set the rules aside: special situations demand different rules, so in highly adverse weather conditions where public transport is cancelled and roads are dangerous, it is not heroic to fight your way to work, risking your life: it is foolish.

The Process of Focused Busyness

We are all influenced by something or someone and, on the matter of focused busyness, like many people, I owe a debt to the leading twentieth century management thinker, Peter Drucker, who distinguished between efficient, which is the ability to do things well, and effective, which is doing the right things well.

Focused busyness therefore starts with finding the right things to do, and then looks for ways to do them well. The first five chapters are about how to create focused busyness.

Compelling Causes

**The world is full of opportunities:
start by focusing on the right ones.**

The world is full of opportunities and a Powerhouse will start by focusing on the right ones – a small number that will give the best results. A Powerhouse will turn them into compelling causes that spur effective action and achieve worthwhile outcomes.

The Three Laws of Opportunity

An opportunity is an uncertain future that could have a valuable, positive outcome. Opportunities are a fundamental part of life and so, like Newton's three laws of motion and the three laws of thermodynamics, there are three laws of opportunity.

The First Law of Opportunity

*'You will get the best results when you focus on
exploiting opportunities: not on solving problems.'*

The Second Law of Opportunity
*'Allocate your time, your energy, and your
resources to your best opportunities.'*

The Third Law of Opportunity
*'Find yourself an environment that is
rich in opportunities.'*

Turn Your Opportunities into Compelling Causes

Frederick the Great, who faced monumental defeats before he was able to expand his kingdom of Prussia, said: 'To defend everything is to defend nothing.'

A Powerhouse needs motivation, and nothing motivates us more powerfully than a cause to pursue. From among all your possible opportunities, find a small number of compelling causes that you can commit yourself to. These should be the opportunities with the potential to deliver the greatest satisfaction or value for the effort you put in. Let these propel you to do your best work and to exclude distractions.

Identify no more than five opportunities to seize. Make them your very best opportunities, because they must compel you to succeed. As US President Abraham Lincoln said:

*'Always bear in mind that your own resolution to succeed is
more important than any one thing.'*

Express Your Compelling Causes as Outcomes

Now express each of these compelling causes as an outcome: *'My cause is to ...'*

You need to decide on no more than five outcomes that will be your focus over the next three months. These will dominate your agenda, keeping your attention on achieving a small number of worthwhile outcomes.

Why five; and why three months? A small number of causes to pursue will result in greater personal effectiveness than a large number for three reasons.

First, it will produce the greater focus that you need, to produce the Powerhouse performance and the spectacular results that you want. With too many causes to pursue, you will dissipate your effort and achieve little of value towards any of the outcomes.

Second, it is unlikely that all of your opportunities will be of the same scale. It is the way of things that a small number of them will, together, deliver the vast majority of the benefit. This is sometimes known as 'The Pareto Principle' after Italian economist, Vilfredo Pareto, who found in early twentieth century Italy that most of the wealth was in the pockets of a small number of people. This is still true today, in all countries and globally. Indeed, the statistic that is best associated with Pareto – that 20 per cent of the population owned 80 per cent of the wealth – is still true, to within a few per cent, of the world today. In a world of near infinite opportunities, you must choose something or risk achieving nothing.

The third reason to pursue a small number of causes is because it is risky. When you decide which causes are truly compelling to you, you are making the choice to abandon a host of other, lesser opportunities. This is risky: what if you choose wrong? But deciding is cutting yourself off from the alternatives and that level of risk should really sharpen your senses, stiffen your sinews and summon up all of your energy: you are committed now.

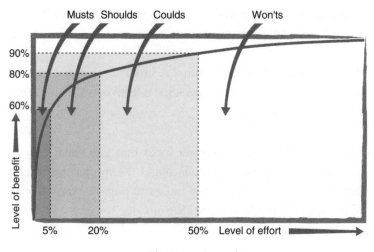

The Pareto Principle

This leads us to the reason why it is best to determine your compelling causes for the next three months – not for the next year. If you choose wrongly, then shorter-term causes mean you can abandon a poor choice more quickly and refocus your efforts. If it is still looking like the right choice after three months of effort and learning, then decide what the next outcome is towards winning this cause.

Express Your Outcomes with Precision

Many writers have written many words about goal setting and most of them focus on the idea of SMART goals. Some have even developed the idea of SMARTER goals – cute! I developed the concept of SMARTEST goals for an earlier book, where SMARTEST stands for:

Specific	Be absolutely precise in stating your intention.
Meaningful	Be clear why you want this outcome.
Action-oriented	Make sure the goal is something you can achieve through your own effort.

Responsible	Check that your intention does not conflict with something else that really matters to you.
Towards	Word your goal so it takes you towards what you want: rather than away from what you don't.
Exciting	Choose goals that will excite you – you may as well.
Supported	Identify the people and resources that can help.
Time-bound	Set a deadline: deadlines are highly motivating both consciously and unconsciously.

But this is not enough for a Powerhouse performer. We need to look at the latest research, and there are three pieces that should transform the way you determine your outcomes.

Experts Do it Differently

In studies of high school basketball players at three levels (expert, non-expert and novice), Timothy Cleary and Barry Zimmerman of the City University of New York found that experts set goals differently from non-experts. Experts set specific goals, like to hit ten out of ten shots, to bend their knees when they throw, or to keep their eye on the rim of the basket. Non-experts and novices also set goals based on the outcome, their technique and their focus, but the goals they set were far more general, like to make their shots, to try harder and to concentrate more.

Lesson 1: Set very specific goals that you can monitor every step of the way, with real precision.

Short-Term and Long-Term Goals

It's official – there is no answer yet to the simple question of whether short or long-term goals work better. The evidence shows that the answer depends on the circumstances. If you have a lot of work to do or a big project, research by Albert Bandura and Dale Schunk suggests that setting yourself intermediate goals will produce better performance. But work by Dutch researchers Maurice de Volder and Willy Lens showed that a focus on the long-term future helped high school students achieve more by seeing the link between day-to-day work and what they wanted from life.

Lesson 2: Set yourself motivating long-term goals and then create simple short-term goals so you can track your progress.

Change 'I Will' to 'Will I?'

We all hold a steady flow of conversation with ourselves, in our heads, but how does the way we talk to ourselves affect how well we achieve our goals? Ibrahim Senay, Dolores Albarracin and Kenji Noguchi looked at the impact of different ways we use our self-talk. They set students challenging puzzles, and compared the impact on solving them of either thinking 'I will solve this', or thinking 'Will I solve this?'

In a series of experiments, their results were as conclusive as they were surprising ...

We have got used to the idea of 'the power of positive thinking' and so you might expect the students who thought positive 'I will ...' thoughts to do better. They did not. Students who thought 'Will I ... ?' consistently out-performed those who thought 'I will ...'. This seems to be an example of a wider phenomenon in the psychology of influence; that questions induce thoughts about the answers to them, and hence triggers intrinsic, self-generated motivation. The authors of the study speculate that the 'I will ...' form takes away some of our sense of control over events, thus reducing our sense of personal responsibility.

Lesson 3: When thinking about your goals, ask yourself 'Will I ...?'

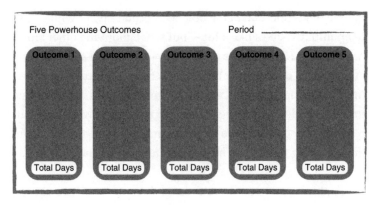

Powerhouse outcomes template

Powerhouse Outcomes

To help you to deliver on your compelling causes, you need to be able to develop your five Powerhouse outcomes, and a simple quarterly outcomes sheet will help you keep them at the front of your mind. You can download a copy of this template at www.beapowerhouse.co.uk. On the five Powerhouse outcomes sheet; make a note of the three-month period that these outcomes cover.

Step 1: A Clear Outcome

For each of your outcomes, give it a motivating title and a short description of what you want to achieve over the three months. This may be a whole outcome, or a step on the way to a larger outcome, so note that down too.

Step 2: Allocate Time to Your Outcomes

Make an estimate of the amount of time each of your outcomes will need. Each quarter will have 65 working days, but you will need three of them to attend to mundane administrative work, which we will cover soon, in the section titled The 5 Per Cent Solution. So allocate between 50 and 60 days across your five Powerhouse outcomes, to allow for some contingency.

People often find that being able to allocate, say, 12 whole days to an initiative feels like a lot – 'but what about the other stuff I have to do? That will get in the way – I won't be able to spend all of the 12 days on it.' Well, that's the secret to Powerhouse time planning: actually spending large chunks of unbroken time on single compelling causes. To achieve Powerhouse outcomes, you need to drive down mundane, administrative and time-wasting tasks to an absolute minimum … and focus.

If you think you need more than 60 days for your five causes, then you have too many outcomes. It is better to do fewer things and do them well, so decide which to drop now, rather than find yourself not achieving what you want or, worse still, delivering poor quality results. An alternative to dropping an outcome is to split it into two stages and set this quarter's outcome as completing Stage 1.

Note that if you have a significant number of days of fixed commitment coming up, like training courses or annual leave, reduce the 50 to 60 days accordingly.

Step 3: Plan Each Outcome in Detail

Now you need to take each of your five Powerhouse outcomes and put some detailed planning in, to create the short-term goals that will allow you to track your progress and celebrate your successes. We often call these 'milestones'. A good way to do this is as a single page in your notebook, or on an outcome specification sheet like the one illustrated below. You can download a copy of this template at www.beapowerhouse.co.uk.

Use your outcome specification sheet to think through the detail of what you are going to be doing, and why. Powerhouse outcomes are worthwhile work, so you will spend a large part of your time on one of three types of activity:

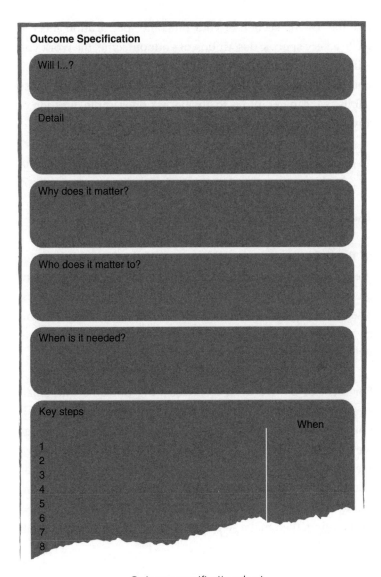

Outcome specification sheet

1. Creative: thinking, imagining and developing new ideas.
2. Constructive: designing, building and getting things done.
3. Relationship-building: talking, listening and helping people.

Use the 'Detail' section of your outcome specification sheet to write a very specific description of your outcome, the work you will be doing, and where you need to apply most attention if you want to succeed. One of the most valuable Powerhouse habits you can get into is to always ask one simple question of anything worthwhile that you plan to do:

> *'What do I need to pay most attention to,*
> *if I want to succeed at this?'*

These are your critical success factors.

In the 'When is it needed?' box, record the final deadline for this Powerhouse outcome. This can stretch well beyond a single quarter and, indeed, some projects can take many years. The outcome you will record on your five outcomes sheet will be a single stage or set of milestones, which you can complete within the quarter.

For most of us, we need to break a big outcome into small steps, just to feel in control and to help us get started. Even if you don't need this motivational push, it still pays to plan (as we'll see in Chapter 3). Think through the key steps, actions or accomplishments along the way, and include as much detail as you like. The most important step is always the first. If you are prone to putting things off, because they seem too complicated or daunting, then make step one (and the next few steps) small and simple.

Saying N.O.

If you are going to apply Powerhouse focus in pursuing a small number of compelling causes, then you will, from time-to-time, need to deal with distractions. In organizations, these usually come from colleagues, asking you to get involved in other, less important pieces of work, or help them with their compelling causes. Some give and take is vital for the smooth running of any organization – and also for the health of your working relationships. Some people's requests will also contribute to your own compelling causes. Others will not.

Evaluate the request carefully and, if you choose to, decline it. For many of us, this is hard. We don't like saying no: it makes us sound grumpy, churlish, uncooperative and negative. We worry how we will be seen, and whether it will destroy our reputation and damage our relationships. Don't. Done properly, a no can be a positive thing.

To make no positive, transform it into a N.O.
– a Noble Objection.

A no becomes a Noble Objection when you do it for the right reasons and you say it in a respectful, courteous way. The right reasons are important – this is not an excuse to decline to do valuable work on behalf of your organization. Instead, it must be a considered choice as to which work is the most valuable. When you get this right, you earn more respect; not less. After all, if you just said yes to everything, you'd soon be perceived as an easy touch. And say N.O. with good grace and courtesy. Let them know that, whilst you have to say no, you don't take any pleasure in it. There is a lot more on when to say no and how to say no, in *The YES/NO Book*.

The 5 Per Cent Solution

The principle of planning for Powerhouse productivity is to use the vast majority of your time for highly worthwhile activities that contribute to your compelling causes, creating changes that matter. This means keeping the time you spend on other things – distractions, maintenance and routine admin – to an absolute minimum.

A maximum of 5 per cent is about right. Since most Power-houses work between eight and 12 hours per day, let's assume you work for ten. This means half an hour per day is all you have for keeping things ticking over and maintaining the infra-structure of your working life. That is two and a half hours per week, or about a day a month. Hence, three days per quarter, as I mentioned above.

It may not sound a lot, but all you need to do in that time is to stay safe, legal and compliant with your organization's require-ments. This stuff doesn't contribute value to your work, so deal with it as quickly and efficiently as you can. Examples might include timesheets, expenses forms and tidying your workspace.

What it does not include are the many low stimulation tasks that feel like admin but are actually a crucial part of deliver-ing value. If you are in sales and you need to write-up notes from a client meeting: then this contributes to a sales outcome. If you come back to the office from a networking meeting with a pocket full of business cards, sending emails to the people you met will contribute to growing your list of valuable con-tacts. If you are a manager or supervisor, then one or more of your objectives are likely to involve team members – because getting the best from them is your job. Reviewing their perfor-mance properly is not admin: it is a part of a compelling cause to improve your team and deliver outcomes.

The Powerhouse Loop

A Continuous Sequence of Steps Towards Powerhouse Effectiveness

It is time to introduce you to the Powerhouse Loop: a continu-ous sequence of steps towards becoming a Powerhouse. It will also help me answer the question of why I recommend you

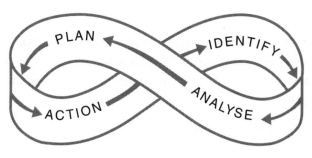

The Powerhouse Loop

to set your five Powerhouse outcomes quarterly and not, for example, annually.

Shift happens; things change. If you focus too closely on one or more outcomes, it is very easy for you to miss a shift in the landscape of your opportunities. If you review everything quarterly, you will be able to reassess your outcomes in the light of what you have achieved, how other things have changed, and your wider aspirations and compelling causes. Too much focus on individual outcomes leads us to miss new opportunities, and even to achieve outcomes yet lose sight of the compelling cause that motivated you to seek it.

Because it is a loop, there is no start or finish, but to describe the Powerhouse Loop we need to start somewhere, and a good place is with 'identify'.

Identify

Here is where you turn up your perception switch to full, and ask:

- 'What is going on?'
- 'What are the opportunities?'

The skills you need are observing, questioning, listening and learning. I will give you the skills you need for this in Chapter 7.

Analyse

You now need to figure out what your observations mean and define the outcomes that will take best advantage of the opportunities open to you. Turn up your judgement switch to full, and ask:

- 'Why is this happening?'
- 'What does it mean?'
- 'Where is my best advantage from it?'

What you need for this stage is to give yourself the time to think through what you have observed, to assess cause and meaning, to form connections and links, and find relationships that will help you to interpret and understand events.

Plan

Planning is about finding solutions and figuring out the answer to:

- 'How can I seize this opportunity?'

The switch you need to turn up at this stage is self-control: you will be tempted to dive in and try to make progress. But the old adage turns out to be true all too often:

> *'Failing to plan is the same as planning to fail.'*

Look at your options and alternatives and evaluate each one for ease of carrying it out, likelihood of success and consequences of failure. Make decisions and figure out the steps you need to take to make your desired outcomes come about.

Action

Now switch productivity to full and focus on implementing your plan, testing and reviewing progress as you go. The questions to ask are:

- 'What if we do this?'
- 'How did this work?'
- 'What next?'

Keep going until either you complete your outcome or it is time to put your head up again, like a meerkat surveying the horizon, and identify any changes that you need to think about.

The Pyramid of Balance

In designing your outcomes, you will want to balance your priorities between getting more, getting it better, getting it sooner and getting it more cheaply. You cannot achieve all of them, but you can decide which are more and which less important for each outcome. The following diagram illustrates your choices.

Let's say for example that your compelling cause is to have better management information for decision-making and your outcome is to develop a new financial management and reporting process.

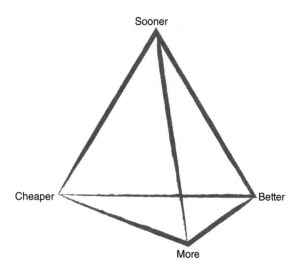

The pyramid of balance: more – better – sooner – cheaper

If you want more information, you will have to either sacrifice quality, take longer to get it, or invest more money and resources in developing systems and gathering information. If you want better quality information, you will need to cut down on the volumes, allow more time to get and collate it, or invest more money and resources in the process. If you want faster access to the information, you can either reduce the amount of information you focus on, allow it to be less reliable, or invest more in getting it. And, if you want your information more cheaply, you must require less of it, accept lower standards or resign yourself to waiting longer.

The more – better – sooner – cheaper diagram will never answer any of your questions, but it will always make your choices startlingly clear.

Staying Sharp

In a clever experiment, John Darley and Daniel Batson demonstrated the dangers of focusing too closely on your immediate outcome and therefore not spotting a valuable opportunity to work towards your compelling cause. The Princeton University researchers asked seminary students to prepare to give a short talk about the story of the Good Samaritan (who stopped to help a man who had been stripped and beaten by thieves).

They then sent the students across campus to deliver the talk, telling them they were late and must hurry. On the way, the students encountered an actor playing a victim. Would the students, with a vocation to help others and the parable of the Good Samaritan in their mind, stop to help? The answer is no. For students with a strong vocation or a weak one, and given a talk about the Good Samaritan or a neutral topic, the results were the same: most failed to stop and help. It was only students who were not told to hurry who were likely to stop and help.

Rushing towards your outcomes frustrates your ability to see and properly evaluate the significance of what is right in front of you. This is why a Powerhouse needs a process for constant re-evaluation. I call it 'The Next Bend' process: once a week, take half an hour and find somewhere you can think – a meeting room, a coffee shop or a park bench. Take nothing but a notebook and pen, and let your mind clear. Let the things you have observed but not noticed emerge from your unconscious mind into your consciousness. Ask yourself:

'What am I missing, that is in front of my eyes?'
'What is coming around the next bend?'

Self-Control: 8 Powerhouse Pointers

1. Focused busyness: do stuff that really makes a difference.
2. Compelling causes: the world is full of opportunities; start by focusing on the right ones.
3. Remember the three laws of opportunity: focus on exploiting opportunities, not on solving problems; allocate your time, energy and resources to your best opportunities; and find yourself an environment rich in opportunities.
4. Setting goals: set motivating long-term goals as well as simple short-term goals so you can track your progress.
5. Say NO effectively: to make no positive, transform it into a N.O. – a Noble Objection.
6. The 5 per cent solution: keep distractions, maintenance and routine admin tasks to 5 per cent of your working day.
7. The Powerhouse Loop: becoming a Powerhouse is a continuous sequence of steps.
8. The next bend: always ask *'What am I missing, that is in front of my eyes?'*

2
Judgement
Do the Right Things for the Right Reasons

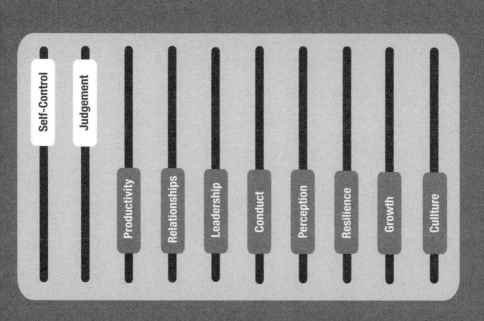

Self-Control

Judgement

Productivity

Relationships

Leadership

Conduct

Perception

Resilience

Growth

Culture

Will you be a *Powerhouse* of value or a whirlwind of destruction? Be sure that your energy has purpose, because success will only come if what you are doing is truly worthwhile. But it is not only you who has to be sure that what you are doing is worthwhile: you have to persuade your bosses that you have made the right choices, to win their endorsement and support.

So being a Powerhouse is not only about doing the right thing: it is also important that you understand why you are doing it, and that you have made your choices for the right reasons.

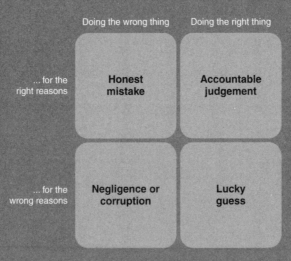

Powerhouse effectiveness: doing the right things for the right reasons

The Algebra of Decision-Making

**Success can only come if what you
are trying to do is worthwhile.**

Does what you want to do make sense? Success can only come if what you are trying to do is worthwhile, so you must assess the pros and cons of your priorities and be able to convince yourself and others that they are truly worthwhile. The most difficult and important decisions will benefit from other people's contributions, but the basic algebra of how to make a good decision is always the same.

A Good Decision

The first and most important thing to know about decisions is this:

A *good* decision is not the same thing as the *right* decision.

We all want to make good decisions, but how can we know if the decision we have just made is a good one? The answer cannot be that it is good if it is correct, because we often cannot know whether it is the right choice until time has passed and events have played out. There must be another way to know if a decision was a good one – whether or not it turns out to be right.

You can assess the quality of your decisions with a simple formula:

Decision Quality = Proof + Process + Perspective + Protection

Four requirements determine how good you decision will be and experience tells us that, the better your decision is, the more likely it is to be right. So you need to understand what each of these elements means and how you can get them right.

1. Proof

The first thing to say about proof is: don't expect absolute certainty. You will rarely achieve it. But what you can achieve is a high standard of evidence that contributes to your decision-making. Unfortunately, some evidence is hard to gather, and some is easy to ignore. The evidence itself is rarely enough, however. It is always accompanied by an interpretation, which can introduce bias.

This leads to three critical questions:

Question 1: What evidence are you missing?

The first thing is to avoid falling into a very common trap: the belief that what you see is all there is. Other evidence can be hidden and hard to reach. So a Powerhouse needs to poke around. When you do, be aware of a second common trap: that supporting evidence is obvious. We spot evidence like trends and events that endorse our point of view much more easily than things that contradict it. Psychologists call this the confirming evidence trap, and it results in not so easily spotting good work by someone whom we think of as a poor performer, yet failing to recognize the mistakes that our most trusted colleagues make. This is called the horns and halo effect.

Question 2: What evidence are you ignoring?

Have you put some evidence in the 'too difficult' folder? Is there something that you noticed, which doesn't fit? Or is the group avoiding talking about the things that cause disagreement, and focusing instead on what you can all easily agree on? Ironically, it is these tricky pieces of evidence that often yield the greatest insights and lead to the best decisions. But tackling them is not easy, so a Powerhouse needs to hunker down and take it on.

Question 3: What evidence are you misinterpreting?

We think of data and evidence as objective; but this is not so. It means nothing until we interpret it; and your interpretation must inevitably involve assumptions, approximations and analysis – all of which can be wrong. A Powerhouse must always ask: 'How else can I interpret this, and what different conclusions would that give me?'

2. Process

You are looking, of course, for an honest evaluation of the evidence, before you make your decision. There are three things that will help you.

Framing the question well

How you frame the question that you need to decide can often bias your consideration of your choices. This is known as the framing trap and its commonest form is whether you frame your choice as being about losses or gains. Here is an example:

Dread disease expected to kill 600 people in our town!

… reads the newspaper headline. Policy-makers want your opinion on two courses of action. Would you support action A or B?

Action A will save 200 lives

Action B has a 1/3 chance of saving all 600 lives and a 2/3 chance of saving none

Now another expert comes along and offers you a new choice. Would you support action C or D?

Action C will lead to 400 deaths

Action D has a 1/3 chance that no one will die and a 2/3 chance that everyone will die

Most people will choose option A over option B, and then will choose option D, rather than option C. What did you choose?

Here is the point: option A is exactly the same as option C and option B, is the same as option D. So why do most choose inconsistent options? The answer lies in the way the choices were framed. The A or B choice was framed as a choice of gains, and we tend to avoid risk in these circumstances: option A offers certainty, against a large chance of saving no one. The C or D choice was framed as a choice of losses, in which case we usually prefer to take risks to minimize those losses. So most people choose option D to avoid the certainty of losing 400 lives.

How you frame a question can influence the choice you will make, so a Powerhouse will always look at their choices through different frames, trying to understand how framing can change the way they see things.

By the way, this is not at all easy: even knowing what you do, can you decide which choice, A and C or B and D is best? I doubt you can.

Respecting the evidence

Even if you have found a neutral way to frame your choice, can you view your evidence with cold objectivity and remove all self-interest from your consideration? This is not to say that self-interest should never be a factor in your decisions, but it will help to understand what component of your thinking is subjective.

If you thought framing and the confirming evidence trap in the section under proof make decision-making hard enough, there is more bad news. These are just the tip of a very large iceberg of biases and traps for the unwary decision-maker, and a Powerhouse needs to be aware of at least five of the more common traps.

The first thing trap: the first opinion stated often frames the discussion and leads to the bias that your decision needs to be based on the extent to which that opinion is right or wrong. Avoid this by deliberately starting a discussion by examining the evidence, and not by stating the opinions. Ask people who are neutral to speak first.

The powerful person trap: powerful people, whether they have formal authority, are widely liked and respected or have deep expertise, can sway opinions disproportionately. Ask them to keep their opinions to late in the discussion. This also helps with …

The loss of face trap: nobody likes to be seen to reverse their opinion, so we often cling to our positions in spite of evidence we are wrong. This is often especially so of powerful people, but if they do not share their opinion, they will find it easier to change their mind, because they will not be seen to do so by everyone else.

The good story trap: when the evidence easily conforms to a set of stereotypes, we get seduced into building a familiar narrative. This is lazy thinking and we often fail to notice logical flaws in our interpretation.

The recent events trap: recent events – particularly startling or significant events – can readily colour our opinions. A train crash immediately changes our subjective perception of the risk of train travel, making it seem far more dangerous than it was yesterday. However, if it were a genuine accident, the risk would remain the same.

Assessing multiple options

One way to avoid a bad decision is to evaluate more than one option. This turns a decision from a dilemma – yes or no – into a genuine choice. More options means more choice, but beware of too many options, leading to over-choice and a real psychological barrier to making a selection. I recommend three to five choices. Avoid three choices if all you are doing is sandwiching a moderate option between two extremes. This is just manipulation.

3. Perspective

When I listed five common decision-making traps above, I could easily have added another:

The emotional response trap: we react emotionally to certain possibilities and threats. Things we don't understand and risks that have a huge impact can affect our judgement of their likelihood. Things that affect family and friends trigger different responses to the same things when they affect strangers. This emotional proximity effect extends further: people from our town 'matter' more than people from far away, and events in our country seem more significant than the same events in a far-off land.

A Powerhouse needs to separate emotions into a different part of their decision-making and the best way to do this is to look at a decision from different points of view. Of course, the ideal way to do this is to involve a range of different people, and to make sure everyone gets properly heard. Here, three things give group decision-making Powerhouse effectiveness:

Diversity: of background, experience and opinion. This is the most valuable asset you can have in making a good decision. But it only helps if you have the next two things ...

Independence: of thought, of analysis and of access to the evidence. As soon as one person produces their analysis, they introduce a bias from their selection of data and how they have interpreted it.

Respect: for different points of view, different experiences and different cultural values. Without this, diversity will be stifled by the prevailing mood. Respect does not mean, however, that you must agree: by all means fight for what you believe, but also listen to what others argue in their own way.

A great tool to help you take multiple perspectives is to deliberately task yourself with assessing the decision in different ways, using the Powerhouse multiple perspectives grid.

The Powerhouse multiple perspectives grid

	How do I see this decision?	How would other people affected see this decision?	How would an impartial observer see this decision?
Logically			
Gut instinct			
Emotionally			
Looking for opportunities			
Aware of risks			
Seeking alternatives			

There is one perspective that must dominate all others: authority. A decision can only be a good one if the decision-maker has the authority to make the decision. In organizations, this is most often the authority that comes with position, but it can also be the authority that comes with experience, expertise or knowledge.

4. Protection

The final condition for a good decision is one we alluded to in the Powerhouse multiple perspectives grid, but we need to put more emphasis on it: risk. For a decision to be a good one, it must take full account of all of the risk: the uncertainties in the outcome of your decision. The problem we face is that we base our decisions on our predictions about the future that follows our choice. And we then believe that prediction and fail to see how things could turn out in other ways. The first step you can take to protect yourself is to evaluate multiple outcomes, or scenarios, following your decision. Don't just look at what you expect to happen, which is often the best case scenario, look at what else could happen – particularly the worst plausible scenario. How does that affect your choice?

When you have done that, if you still think this is the best decision, you will need to think through what you can do to mitigate the threats. I won't say any more about this now, because there is a whole section, Spotting the Risks, of Chapter 7 dedicated to the topic of spotting and handling risks.

The Poetry of Persuasion

A decision is nothing if you cannot sell it.

A Powerhouse needs to get things done, and a decision is the necessary first step. But a decision is nothing if you cannot sell it.

We sell ideas mostly with words, and sometimes with pictures or experiences. This is the art of persuasion.

Like poetry, good persuasion is characterized by:

- A careful choice of words (or images, or experiences).
- Thoughtful sequencing and positioning of your words (or images or experiences).
- An appeal to the different interests of your audience.
- Selection from a range of techniques that give your words (or images or experiences) eloquence and power.

Poetry has metre, rhythm and metaphor: persuasion has trust, reason and emotion. To persuade others, they must see you as dependable, reasonable and moving.

Trust

To build trust, you have to show me three things: that you know what you are talking about, that you understand what matters to me, and that you have integrity and will honour your commitments. This gives a Powerhouse three areas to work on.

1. Knowing What You Are Talking About

In your chosen area of expertise, build your skills and knowledge. To adopt a new skill set from nothing takes no more than access to information and the discipline to practice. Let's say you want to learn to write computer programs or develop websites. Get yourself a couple of good tutorial books aimed at beginners and set aside a couple of hours a day. Maybe that means getting up a couple of hours earlier each day – or maybe foregoing television or trips to the pub in the evening. In those two hours, do the exercises as prescribed and work steadily through the learning materials. Two hours a day isn't much, especially if you take weekends off. But over the course of a month, that is 44 hours of weekday study.

2. One of Us

If I don't believe you understand my perspectives and care about them, why should I agree with you or help you? You will boost your persuasiveness massively when you have made friends with the people you want to influence; when we like and trust you and feel that you are one of us.

3. A Reputation for Integrity

One simple mis-step can destroy your reputation, so as well as building up your reputation for integrity, you must also look after it with care. You can speed up the process of building my trust in you by showing me how people I already trust also trust you. Consequently, testimonials and personal recommendations are powerful reputation-builders. You can also speed your reputation along by taking on more responsibilities and meeting them. But beware: too many and you will run the risk of failing and, if you fail just once, you will give yourself a huge new mountain to climb.

Reason

We looked at the importance of reason in the earlier sections on proof and process, under The Algebra of Decision-Making. Deploying reason to help you persuade is necessary, but it is never enough. People aren't persuaded by reason: they use it to help them feel good about the choice they have made. But you do need to get reason right and, in the poetry of persuasion, that means three things:

1. You have the evidence.
2. Your argument makes sense.
3. I understand your argument.

The important one here is number three: it is no good making a strong argument if I don't understand you. We all tend to talk about things in a way that makes sense to ourselves.

To persuade me, you must describe your argument in a way that makes sense to me.

Emotion

Emotions are funny old things! We value them in our private lives yet tend to ignore them and hope they will go away when we are at work. They won't. When we make a decision, we typically start by asking ourselves 'Can I trust you?' If the answer is yes, your reasoning may give me the justification for my decision, but I will make my decision based on emotion; usually for one of three reasons:

1. I Care About it (Sympathy)

Use personal examples and stories to engage my emotions and make me feel for the situation of others. This is what charities focus on to engage us. Like them, you can turn arguments and presentations into powerful personal stories.

2. It Feels Right (Values)

Appeal to what is most important to me, and to my sense of who I am and what I stand for. This is what politicians focus on. Like them, you can base your arguments on our need to act in ways that we believe are right – or to avoid doing what we perceive as wrong.

3. I Feel Compelled to (Psychology)

Harness the way my brain works to make me want to agree. This is what advertisers and marketers focus on. Like them, you can use your understanding of psychology to motivate my decision choice. Here are seven powerful techniques that advertisers use. See which ones you can spot in the adverts when you next watch TV or read a magazine.

1. Because I want it …
   Crude but effective: appeal to my greed, desire or self-interest.

2. Because I am scared …

   Show me the consequences of not saying yes and fear will do the rest.

3. Because you know what you are talking about …

   Get an independent expert to advocate for the case you are making.

4. Because I promised …

   Show how your recommendation is consistent with something I have already said, done or committed myself to.

5. Because I owe you …

   If you have done me favours in the past, or made concessions to me, gently remind me and I will feel the urge to return the favour.

6. Because it's the easy decision …

   Set out a few options, but make the others less convenient, less affordable, less effective or less secure. I'll always go for the easy choice.

7. Because you've worn me down …

   Professional salespeople know that persistence and flexibility pay. If you can't persuade me today, adapt your approach and try again tomorrow. As you and your proposal become more familiar, eventually, I may say yes.

Notice how all of these techniques have one thing in common. If you want to persuade me, you must give me a 'because'. If you don't, I will have no way to justify my decision to my colleagues or myself. In that case, perhaps it would be safer to say no. With a good juicy 'because' in my pocket, I can persuade others that my decision was a good one.

The Geometry of Change

The right decision yesterday may be the wrong thing to do today.

Life would be so simple for a Powerhouse if you could make your decision, get it endorsed, and then work towards your outcome until it gets done. But the universe is rarely that friendly to us, and the right decision yesterday may turn out to be the wrong thing to pursue today. Shift happens!

Let's say you picked a project to pursue for all of the right reasons. Two things can make it the wrong thing today: changes in your project, or changes in the rest of the world.

Changes in Your Project

When you do new things, you cannot expect them always to turn out as you planned. You are going to learn new things, you will experiment and sometimes fail, you may test your assumptions and find them wrong. As you do all of this, your understanding will increase and your estimates will improve. You will discover problems and you will often solve them. But sometimes you won't be able to – at least not in a cost or time-effective manner.

Changes in the World

Your external environment is constantly changing; whether it is through commercial, technical, regulatory, economic or social changes. Events can occur or you may notice things you had not spotted before. So you investigate and you start to make connections that you had not made before or begin to understand things more deeply or more clearly. The opportunities that were there previously, or the compelling drivers for change, may have shifted.

Changes in your project, or changes in the world, can mean that what was the right decision yesterday may not be right today. And if you act as if it is still the right decision … you could make a costly mistake. A Powerhouse knows that:

The only way to be right all of the time is to spot when you are wrong quickly … and to change your mind.

The geometry of change

Checkpoints

To make this work, let's return to the Powerhouse Loop from Chapter 1. Between each step, we will introduce a checkpoint.

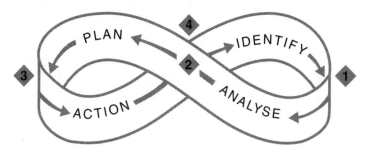

Checkpoints on the Powerhouse Loop

Checkpoint 1: Reality Check

We ask: *'Is there a real opportunity?'* This is your chance to assess whether a seductive idea really does have the potential to be worthwhile analysing in detail.

Checkpoint 2: Sense Check

We ask: *'Does this make good sense?'* By now, you should have understood your opportunity fully and defined what it is and what it is not. In an organizational context, does it make good business sense? How well does it align with your priorities and overall strategy? Does it offer a good return on the time, money and resources you will need to invest? How does it compare with other opportunities that are competing for that time, that money and those resources?

Checkpoint 3: Rigour Check

We ask: *'Are we likely to succeed?'* Following careful planning, you have a budget, a schedule and a method. Now you can assess how confident you are that you can get the outcome you need and that the benefits really do outweigh the risks and costs.

Checkpoint 4: Outcome Check

We ask: *'What was the outcome?'* When you have taken action, did you get what you expected and is it still what you need? Is it 'fit for purpose?' If not, identify the gap and continue around the loop.

The Powerhouse Loop doesn't just work at the level of a whole outcome. Use it and the idea of checkpoints for small components of each initiative, to constantly remain mindful of the possibility that what was once a good idea may no longer be so.

Judgement: 9 Powerhouse Pointers

1. Worthwhile choices: success can only come if what you are trying to do is worthwhile.
2. A *good* decision is not the same thing as the *right* decision.
3. Decision Quality = Proof + Process + Perspective + Protection.
4. How you frame the question can often bias your consideration of your choices.
5. A decision is nothing if you cannot sell it.
6. Poetry has metre, rhythm and metaphor: persuasion has trust, reason and emotion.
7. Shift happens! The right decision yesterday may be the wrong thing to do today.
8. The only way to be right all of the time is to spot when you are wrong quickly … and to change your mind.
9. Use the Powerhouse Loop to make a regular Reality Check, Sense Check, Rigour Check and Outcome Check.

3
Productivity
Do the Right Things Right

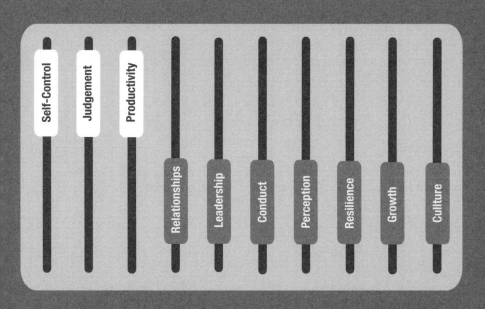

Productivity keeps the heart of a **Powerhouse** beating. We'll look at the source of your productive energy, and the reasons you can be super-effective in the way you use the time available.

Before you dive into action, planning and preparation are everything. There is a whole host of tools available to you that are neither difficult to use nor require special equipment or software. In this chapter, we'll look at how you can give yourself and others the confidence that you know what you are doing and you have the resources you need … and how you can be efficient in your use of the time available.

And when you have finished what you are doing, don't let the last few details compromise your effectiveness. Power down with proper postparation.

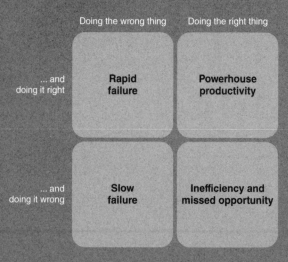

Powerhouse effectiveness: doing the right things right

The Source of Power: Planning

**Planning frees up the mental capacity for a Powerhouse
to focus fully on what you choose to tackle.**

The Zeigarnik effect, named after Russian Psychologist Bluma
Zeigarnik, describes the way uncompleted tasks continue to
nag at us, robbing us of mental focus. A huge 'To Do List' can
be a big distraction. Recently, EJ Masicampo has uncovered an
important new insight into the Zeigarnik effect: the distraction
of an unfinished task can be allayed, not just by completing it,
but by planning how you will do it. Planning frees up the mental capacity for you to focus fully on what you choose to tackle.

Escape the 'To Do Tyranny'

A simple To Do List is not a plan; it is a list of things that are
bugging you. If it is your only time management tool, then it
is likely to be having a toxic effect on your productivity and
maybe even on your life – even if you consider yourself good at
ticking or crossing stuff off it.

Think about the end of the day: the budding Powerhouse is
productive, so you have been constantly completing to do
items through your day. But you have probably also been adding new ones as you go. So now it is time to finish, but there's

still stuff on the list. Do you: a) stay late and finish the list, leaving you tired and resentful; or b) go home, leaving you worried about tomorrow's workload? As a one-off choice, there is little problem, but as a lifestyle, in which the same thing happens nearly every night … it is a recipe for stress and exhaustion: it is certainly not Powerhouse effectiveness.

You need to turn your impotent To Do list into a potent planning tool, and tame its infinite growth, by converting it into a closed 'Today List' of things you will do today, before finishing your work and going home satisfied. A sense of progress is one of the most rewarding aspects of work.

The Powerhouse Planning Process

The Powerhouse planning process always starts with knowing what outcomes you want. We looked at this, over a longer period, in Chapter 1. Now let's think about tomorrow and follow a simple five-minute routine for planning your work.

First: Outcomes

Look at your diary: what commitments are already fixed? Think about tomorrow: what level of interruption or disruption do you anticipate. Now ask yourself: how much time are you likely to have, undisturbed, to pursue the worthwhile outcomes you want?

Starting with your current list of compelling causes and any outstanding items on your To Do List, decide what outcomes to choose for tomorrow. Select the right amount to fit into the time available. It is likely to be a small number: one, two or three at most.

Second: Activities

From your list of outcomes, create a Today List of things you will do to create those outcomes. You can put your To Do List to one side now. It has only one function: to act as a store of ideas for things you might want to do, to save you from having to remember them. A better name is therefore a 'Might Do List'.

Third: Times

Think about how long each of your activities will take you. Don't worry about being precise, but focus instead on being confident: set a time that is challenging and will require full Powerhouse effectiveness – but not one that is unrealistic and would need superhuman capabilities.

Think about what resources you will need, and when they will be available. This may be equipment or materials, significant assets or other people. Completing your planning will take longer if you need to consult others about their involvement in helping you achieve your outcomes.

Fourth: Schedule

This step is vital. Schedule your activities into your day, starting with the biggest ones. Of these, put the toughest, most complex, work into the prime time slots when you are at your mental and physical best. Because we deplete our energy and willpower during the day, for most of us, the best slot is at the start of our working day: as I type this sentence, it is still before 7 am. All of your activities – perhaps clustered into groups – should now be in an outline plan for your day. The gaps in your day plan allow for responding to urgent requests, or for your 5 per cent time.

Your OATS Plan

These four steps: Outcomes, Activities, Times and Schedule, form your OATS plan. Don't just do this daily; at the end of each week, sketch out your plan for next week. Here is the format a typical weekly OATS plan takes.

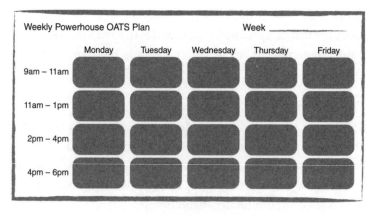

A weekly Powerhouse OATS plan

You can also plan a month at a time with an OATS plan, but always review it weekly, and then review your plans again daily. Each review need take only five minutes or less.

What Goes Wrong With Plans

The second biggest planning failure is to believe your plan.

Our planning often lets us down, so to avoid some of the common mistakes, here is a Powerhouse list of ten common things that go wrong with plans and what you can do about each of them.

1. Planning Fallacy

Perhaps the commonest cause of plans going wrong is the tendency to under-estimate the time, cost or resources needed. This is due to over-optimism about what you can achieve.

Solution: Red team review. Ask someone else (or a team of people when dealing with a large, complex plan) to review your plans with a sceptical eye. While we all typically over-estimate what we can achieve, most of us equally have a more realistic view of what others can do.

2. History Neglect

Another common failure is not looking back and learning from the lessons of the past, leading us to repeat the same mistakes. Doh.

Solution: A deliberate process of reviewing all relevant recollections, records and data.

3. Narrow Focus

If you focus too much on your own tasks, you can find yourself ignoring external factors that will impinge on what you are doing.

Solution: Put your head over the wall and look around at what else is happening in your team, your organization, and your social and commercial environment. Ask what trends can affect what you are doing. There will be much more on this in Chapter 7, Reading the Situation.

4. Competition Neglect

Related to narrow focus, one specific source of planning error is to ignore the actions of other people or organizations that are, in some way, competing with you. It is in their interests to seize resources, misrepresent your situation, or to change the environment in which you are operating. While narrow focus refers to benign or neutral forces, competition neglect addresses potentially malevolent interests.

Solution: Consider role-playing a simulation, taking the perspective of a potential competitor, to identify their possible strategies and how they may affect your initiative.

5. Illusion of Control

Two things combine to create the illusion of control: the tendency to ignore events and forces that are out of your control and focus only on those that you can determine, and the belief that we can control events that are, in fact, outside our control.

Solution: Look for the critical point where your plan can fail and focus on that. Control what you can control and monitor everything else constantly, so you are ready to act on any changes.

6. Murphy's Arrogance
Murphy's Law says that *'if anything can go wrong – it will go wrong'*. Murphy's arrogance is acting as if you are special; as if Murphy's Law does not apply to you.

Solution: Conduct a pre-mortem. Before you finalize your plan – and certainly before you start work on it – think about everything that could go wrong and amend your plan to deal with each possibility, according to its seriousness.

7. Hero Pressure
Have you ever succumbed to the temptation to accept a heroic – but impossible – challenge? That's hero pressure. It may bring out the best in us, in some ways, but succumbing also leads to wasted effort.

Solution: It is hard to spot hero pressure until it is too late. But your friends and colleagues can see it coming and recognize in you the tell-tale signs. The solution is therefore to adopt a trusted colleague to act as a critical friend or mentor, to say: 'hey, look out!'

8. Requirement Creep
The world changes, people change their minds or realize they got it wrong. Some people even take any opportunity to take advantage. You have a project … Then 'could you just …' are the three words you fear above all others.

Solution: Constantly review what is needed proactively and, when needs change or new opportunities arise, evaluate them.

9. Complexity Effect

We often underestimate the time, budget and resources that we will need to cope with the complexity of inter-dependencies. Unlike narrow focus, where we don't see the complexities, here we just over-simplify them. The complexity effect kicks in as soon as people need to work together, or you need cooperation from other agencies.

Solution: Where you can, simplify, and where you cannot, build in contingency.

10. Black Swans

Nassim Nicholas Taleb named the Black Swan effect in his book of the same name. It stands for those unknowable future events that sometimes catch us out. The planning risk is that you focus on what you know and are over-confident in your belief that all you know is all there is to know.

Solution: In the face of uncertainty and rapid change, the most valuable single piece of information is your goal: what matters most. In military language, this is the 'commander's intent' and gives every officer the context within which to make decisions in the face of changed circumstances and an inability to communicate with their commander.

I have offered ten solutions on a one-to-one basis, matching each to a single planning problem. But each solution can address multiple problems and each problem can deserve several fixes. Planning is one of the most important secrets to success, so if all of this sounds a little off-putting, remember this:

The biggest planning failure is to fail to plan.

Power-Up: Preparing

Whenever the results you get depend on the quality of your performance; it pays to prepare.

Whenever the results you get depend on the quality of your performance, it pays to prepare. Musicians and actors rehearse, painters mix their paints, scientists re-set their apparatus, and sportspeople warm up.

So why would you not prepare for the meetings, presentations and events on which your success depends? Too often people treat these as routine, heading off without even thinking about them in advance, beyond checking the time and place in their diary. This is not the Powerhouse way.

If you carry on this way, the results you get will not improve and you will be left wondering why it's never you who gets the promotion. The 'one last push' strategy for success can only work if you can find the right direction to push in, and if you keep pushing in the same direction, then why should it work today if it was wrong yesterday?

As part of your planning, plan for the preparation time you need, to ensure you can take best advantage of the opportunity that any event can offer you. Also plan to be there early, so you can do your 'immediate preparation' – the last few minutes of calming your mind, checking your appearance and gathering your thoughts, just before show time.

Powerhouse Moments

Powerhouse moments are the special times you get between events: waiting for a meeting, sitting on a bus or walking to work, for example. These are your chance to mentally prepare for what is coming up. They are the perfect time for thinking, because there need be nothing else to occupy your mind.

Power On: Performing

Effective action defines a Powerhouse.

For all of your planning and preparation, it is effective action that defines a Powerhouse. This means doing one thing at a time, step-by-step, in an orderly way.

One Thing at a Time

If a thing is worth doing, it is worth doing effectively; so don't be tempted into the multi-tasking trap. As soon as you try to do two things at once, two factors click into place: your performance slows down and it becomes less accurate. And if you are a woman, don't be tempted to think this does not mean you. Whilst some limited evidence has recently emerged that, on certain simple tasks, women are better than men at multi-tasking, all that this really means is that you are less bad at it. Multi-tasking is not effective.

Step-by-Step

Two researchers, Teresa Amabile and Steven Kramer, have discovered something most of us suspected for a long time: if we feel we have had a day of making good progress with our work, we finish happy. If we feel that we have achieved little, we leave work miserable. After analysing over 12,000 entries in people's work diaries, they discovered that a sense of progress has the biggest impact on satisfaction at work.

This has simple but profound implications for how to create Powerhouse effectiveness. You need to create the conditions for you and your team members to make progress. So here is a four-part guide to step-by-step Powerhouse performance.

Part 1: Break Your Work Down into Individual Tasks

The tool we use to do this is called the Work Breakdown Structure, or WBS. You divide your outcome into the big areas of work you need to carry out, and then divide each of those into its component jobs. Further divide the jobs into smaller activities, until each activity is a single, coherent task. The diagram shows this schematically, alongside is the way we write it down.

Part 2: Set Milestones for When Tasks Need to be Achieved by

The more milestones you set to indicate the completion of worthwhile tasks, the greater sense of progress you and your team will have.

Part 3: Create the Environment for Achieving Progress

For Powerhouse working with a team, you need to create an environment where your team can achieve Powerhouse productivity. This means ensuring that each person has the resources and skills that they need to do their work, and the level of backup and guidance to feel valued and supported. The combination of resource constraints, frustrating workplace infrastructure and a lack of support creates the toxic conditions where progress is hard to achieve and only happens despite the situation we find ourselves in.

For a Powerhouse working alone, you need to provide yourself with the right environment: gather your resources, optimize your infrastructure and give yourself the mental boost of self-confidence, by focusing on your own skills, experience and determination to succeed.

Create marketing campaign
1. Analyse market
1.1 Product differentiators
1.2 Customer base
1.3 Key competitors
1.4 Buying priorities
2. Determine channel strategy
2.1 Customer patterns
2.2 Cost per impression
2.3 Conversion rates
2.4 Lead times
3. Creative ideas
3.1 Key messages
3.2 Initial ideas
3.3 Idea selection
3.4 Idea refinement
4. Build campaign assets
4.1 Develop message
4.2 Develop artwork
4.3 Create materials
4.4 Review materials

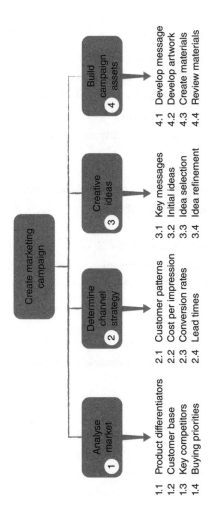

Work Breakdown Structure

Part 4: Mark Progress So You All Notice it

When you achieve a result – mark it. There is a reason why reward charts are a powerful motivator to children and the truth is that most adults would find them motivating too. Create a progress dashboard that allows you to track your own and your team's successes, and display it prominently. Even a list of milestones on a noticeboard, crossed-off daily, will work.

In an Orderly Way

Powerhouse effectiveness requires a conducive work environment and, for most of us, this means orderly. If that's the way you choose to go (and I do recommend it) then the best solution is the 5S Methodology, developed by Hiroyuki Hirano. It was one of the mainstays of Japanese manufacturing and is now at the heart of production processes in many of the world's finest businesses.

Become obsessive about your workplace – clutter-free, with resources ready at hand.

A disorganized workplace leads to lost documents, duplicate effort, delays and frustration, inconsistency, forgotten tasks, stress and general ineffectiveness. This is not what a Powerhouse signs up for.

The 5S arises from five Japanese words that start with an s sound. Happily, each also has a reasonable translation to an English word also starting with s.

1. Seiri – Sort

Tidy up and reduce the amount of stuff you have around you, so that there is nothing unnecessary to your productivity or your emotional and physical wellbeing. This means throwing away anything that is truly not needed and then moving things according to a hierarchy of need:

- Need it every day: keep it close to hand.
- Need it once a week: keep it accessible nearby.
- Need it once a month: store it nearby.
- Need it a few times a year: store it in your least accessible storage.
- Need it less often: archive it with a 'destroy by' date on it.

2. Seiton – Systematize

An orderly workplace means that the crucial resources that you need to do your job are not just ready at hand, but can easily be found and put back. Everything needs its own place and should be properly labelled.

3. Seiso – Sweep

Keep your workspace neat, tidy and clean. Not only does this reinforce the work you have already done sorting and systematizing, but the act of tidying and cleaning can give you a sense of control over your workspace, reducing unwanted stress levels.

4. Seiketsu – Standardize

Within a workplace, procedures and processes ensure that things are done the same way everywhere, reducing the scope for mistakes and poor quality work. For a Powerhouse, the process of standardizing how you do repetitive tasks will make you more efficient at the 5 per cent stuff, and increase your mental capacity for creativity, productivity and effectiveness.

5. Shitsuke – Sustain

Shitsuke is about the discipline to follow your routines and maintain your workplace for peak effectiveness. What you will find is that constant repetition will create habit. Replacing unproductive habits with new ones is far easier than trying to drop unwanted habits. Start your 5S journey today.

Some Thoughts About Procrastination

A Powerhouse shuns pointless procrastination – putting stuff off because you can't be bothered, or because you can't face it right now. We will take a look at how to overcome this in a minute, but first, let's look at two times when procrastination is an effective part of your Powerhouse strategy.

Purposeful procrastination is when you put something off so that you can do something else instead. This may be more important, more urgent, or you may just be inspired. As long as what you are doing is equally worthwhile, this can be an effective strategy.

So too can be purposive procrastination, which is putting something off because there will be a better time to tackle it. Acting now sounds dynamic and effective, but sometimes instant action can lead to poor decisions, lack of consultation, or simply not being able to access all of the right resources.

If, however, there is no benefit in delay, procrastination is bad. Here are the Powerhouse super seven strategies:

1. Willpower is at its peak when you are fresh: schedule it for first thing.
2. Big tasks instil fear: break the task into smaller chunks. Do the first one.
3. Procrastination is harder if you have made a promise: promise it.
4. Aim for adequate: split the task into first and second drafts. Adequate is easy, the polish is in the second draft.
5. Ask for help: working together is often easier.
6. Promise yourself a reward.
7. Set a time limit and work like a dervish.

Power-Down: Postparing

Prepare = Pre (Before) + Pare (Make ready) = Make ready in advance
Postpare = Post (After) + Pare (Make ready) = Make ready after

Your meeting was valuable. You set aside an hour and it was a worthwhile investment in time. It resulted in three things you need to do ... but they'll have to wait, because you have another meeting straight away. This is a crazy, but familiar, scenario to many a would-be Powerhouse. Always follow up from any meeting, event or commitment and, ideally, schedule time to do it as close to the event as possible.

Success often comes when we do the basics well and we follow up. Without the follow up, we squander the benefit of our earlier investment. If you make a commitment: keep it. If someone gives you a commitment: check-up on their progress. If someone helps you: thank them. And if they are working for you: offer feedback.

Do as much of your follow up as you can in person. Email, the default approach for most people, is efficient but not always effective. It rarely enhances relationships and often gets overlooked. If it matters a lot, choose something else: the phone, a handwritten note or a personal visit.

The ultimate in postparation is celebration. On a personal level, a Powerhouse should always celebrate their successes. When you do that, you notice them and feel better about yourself.

This gives you a little more confidence in your abilities, leading you to perform a little better next time. Better performance makes for greater effectiveness and greater effectiveness leads to better results. Better results lead to more success. And when you get more success, you can celebrate again. It is a virtuous cycle: celebration creates success.

Productivity: 9 Powerhouse Pointers

1. Planning frees up the mental capacity for a Powerhouse to focus fully on what you choose to tackle.
2. Escape the To-Do Tyranny: work from a Today List.
3. The biggest planning failure is to fail to plan.
4. The second biggest planning failure is to believe your plan.
5. Whenever the results you get depend on the quality of your performance; it pays to prepare.
6. Performing: effective action defines Powerhouse.
7. Do one thing at a time and step by step: break things down into individual tasks, set milestones, create an environment for progress, and mark your progress.
8. Become obsessive about your workplace – clutter-free, with resources ready at hand.
9. Postpare: make ready after.

4
Relationships
Work With the People Around You

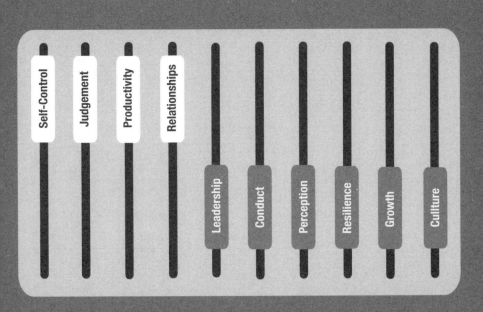

Self-Control
Judgement
Productivity
Relationships
Leadership
Conduct
Perception
Resilience
Growth
Culture

When you have achieved your compelling causes, who will get to determine whether you have been successful or not? There will be a whole range of people, and maybe groups and institutions, who have an interest in what you are doing. How will you win their support and commitment, manage their expectations, and counter any resistance or opposition you meet?

You need to build a *Powerhouse* of connections with people who can help you. Their judgement of your outcomes will determine your true effectiveness. But there is more. To be effective in the face of adversity, a Powerhouse also needs resilience and, whilst this is principally a topic for Chapter 8, human connections are one of the most powerful ways to mitigate the damaging effects of stress.

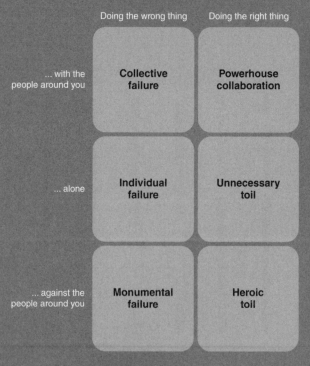

Powerhouse effectiveness: doing the right things, working with the people around you

Strategic Networking

Strategic networking is the process of transforming your relationships with the people around you into long-term assets.

The quality of your relationships with the people around you has been referred to as your 'social capital'. Just like other forms of capital; you can grow your social capital through effort and investment. You grow it when you increase trust, links between people and the flow of information. These often happen in those small moments of learning, inspiration, support and motivation, where we feel a sense of shared triumph.

A Powerhouse can aim to build their social capital through constant repetition of four processes.

Process 1: Understand the power structure.

Process 2: Attract people to you.

Process 3: Create your reputation.

Process 4: Build alliances.

Process 1: Understand the Power Structure

A Powerhouse needs to know where the power lies in one's organization and beyond. A simple way to chart this out is to draw a network of contacts between all of the organization's important people, which highlights who influences who else. For the people you most need to influence, find out who influences them. By getting to know those influencers, you will be able to exert indirect influence.

Think about power in all of its forms, not just the power some people have due to their position in the organization. People can have power from their connections to others, their knowledge or expertise, their access to vital resources, or by their strength of personality and character.

And don't forget that a Powerhouse needs to think long term: some of the young, junior colleagues of today will become the powerful players of tomorrow. Invest in these relationships when they see you as a potential help to them, and you can easily build long-term relationships that you can benefit from in years to come. This will always be a portfolio investment. You cannot know which of your four junior colleagues will one day become a CEO, an influential commentator, a middle manager, or adopt an alternative career.

Process 2: Attract People to You

People like people who are:

- Like themselves.
- Like they want to be.
- Familiar to them.
- Inspiring.
- Enthusiastic.
- Helpful.
- Confident.
- Make them feel good about themselves.

Each of these offers a way to grow the strength of your magnetic personality. People who set themselves apart are rarely liked unless they have something very special to offer. We like people who get involved and clearly understand us. They fit in socially and culturally, but a Powerhouse may want to dress and act half a notch ahead of their peers, to come across as being at the top of the aspirational pile. The more we know someone, in general, the more we like them. So spend time with the people you want to build relationships with.

We are also attracted to confidence and inspirational behaviours, so walk tall, smile and be prepared to articulate a positive vision for what can be. Be enthusiastic and helpful to people and make them feel good about themselves by endorsing their ideas and complimenting them on their achievements. Be generous with praise and thoughtful about what you criticize, so that everything you say will make me think that that I am better off for having heard it.

Process 3: Create Your Reputation

'You can't build a reputation on what you are going to do.'
Henry Ford

A Powerhouse knows that reputations are built on effectiveness. This is not about impressing people in the hope that they will help you in the future. It is about finding ways to be useful to the people you want to influence, so they will remember that they can depend on you.

Think about what reputation you want, so you can put your emphasis in the right place. For example, you may want a reputation as an ideas-generator, a morale-booster, a get-things-done person, as always receptive and positive, or as a source of knowledge and insight. You cannot develop all of these, but you can put your efforts into some of them and work hard to create a reputation that fits your personality and attracts and retains the right people.

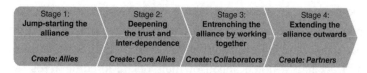

The four stages of building alliances

Process 4. Build Alliances

Building long-term professional alliances is a four-stage process. As you progress from one stage to the next, you convert me first into an ally, then into a core ally, then to your collaborator, and finally to your partner.

Stage 1: Jump-Starting the Alliance

The way you treat someone right at the start of a professional relationship will dictate not just whether, but how quickly, you can build an alliance. Four things you can do are:

1. Presume the other person has earned their position in the organization, and trust their expertise and knowledge.
2. Agree on a shared set of goals and outcomes, and on how you will share any recognition and rewards from working together.
3. Define clear roles for each of you, and how you will interact to share information and collaborate where your roles intersect.
4. Focus on action and making progress. Take responsibility for your tasks and respond quickly to requests for help or support.

Stage 2: Deepening the Trust and Inter-Dependence

Perhaps the strongest way to deepen trust is the 'paying it forward' principle. Doing un-asked-for favours and acting generously to other people will not only build their trust, but also increase their willingness to help you in the future.

Exchanging favours is also a way that we humans enhance our social status, becoming more influential with our peers. This will give you greater social capital. But a Powerhouse has one objective at the top of their mind: effectiveness. And research by Francis Flynn at Stanford University showed that workers who did slightly more giving of favours than receiving were more productive, in terms of completion of tasks, meeting of deadlines and avoidance of mistakes.

When it comes to favours, it is better to give than to receive.

... as long as you don't skew the balance too far, and end up becoming a serial helper with no time for your own work. Choose what favours to grant and then have the confidence to ask for favours when you need them. People around you will sense the balance of your favour giving and receiving and, if they know you to be generous with your time and support, they will be well disposed to you when you need help.

Stage 3: Entrenching the Alliance by Working Together

The nature of collaboration is openness to do whatever it takes to achieve our agreed outcome. It requires high levels of mutual trust and commitment to a shared compelling cause. There is no 'my job and your job; my reward and your reward': there is just 'our jobs and our rewards'.

The benefits, of course, go way beyond the relationship, giving greater problem solving capacity, enhanced judgement and decision-making, and more effective working to deliver greater productivity. The cost is the time and energy it takes to reach and maintain this level of cooperation.

Stage 4: Extending the Alliance Outwards

Once you have created a number of collaborative relationships, a Powerhouse will have the skills to extend this throughout your organization. If you can become the sort of person who lifts up other people's mood, encouraging and energizing them, then you will see the people around you become more motivated and productive.

When you can engage others like you, you can create Positive Energy Networks (PENs) where people find support for their own Powerhouse performance. Linking into a PEN makes people feel energized, creative and powerful. The ultimate social capital comes to those bright suns who sit at the centre of a solar system of Powerhouse performers.

A Tactical Campaign

For short-term stakeholders in your compelling causes, you need a simple, pragmatic and less strategic approach.

Your time is limited and, much as you may want to, you will not be able to invest the time and effort to create long-term relationships with all the people you need to engage, work with and win the support of. For the more peripheral or short-term stakeholders in your compelling causes, you need a simpler, more pragmatic and less strategic approach. Once you establish a new outcome to pursue, follow these three steps to engaging with them constructively.

Step 1: Identify and analyse the interested parties.

Step 2: Plan and manage your campaign.

Step 3: Put your network to work.

We will look at each step in turn.

1. Identify and Analyse the Interested Parties

First, list everyone who has any interest in your compelling cause and its outcome. These may be people affected by what you are doing or people who can in some way affect your outcome or your choices along the way. These are your stakeholders. Now analyse them, using a simple table similar to the following.

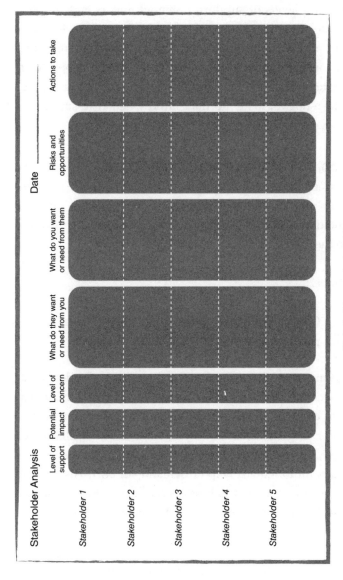

Stakeholder analysis table

This approach will help you to prioritize your actions. The two obviously important groups are your anchor supporters, who are high on levels of support, potential impact and concern, and your potential saboteurs, who also have high levels of concern and impact, but are opposed to what you are doing. A third important group are your fence-sitters: people with moderate to high levels of concern and potential impact, but who have not yet made up their mind whether to support or oppose you.

2. Plan and Manage Your Campaign

The actions to take column in the previous template is where you can record your first thoughts about strategy for each stakeholder. Now put together a communication plan like the one in the following table.

Remember:

Communication is not just about information: you need to win over hearts as well as minds.

Design messages that appeal to the three factors we looked at in the section The Poetry of Persuasion in Chapter 2: trust, reason and emotion. Think carefully about the tone you wish to adopt for each stakeholder: do you want to be conciliatory or assertive, do you want to raise questions or dictate answers, or do you want to request help or demand support? Also decide which medium will appeal best to each stakeholder, balancing the speed and ease of some media, like email, with the greater power of others, like face-to-face meetings.

And don't forget the importance of getting feedback, so you can re-evaluate your strategy and plans if they are not producing the results you want.

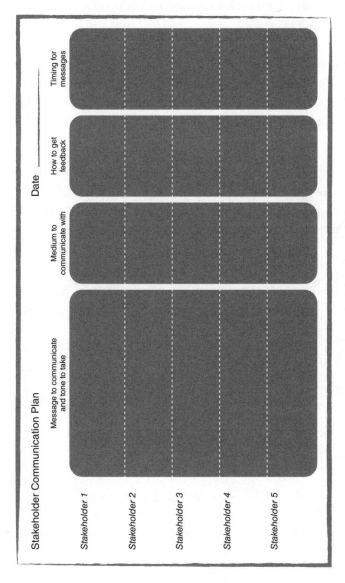

Stakeholder communication plan

3. Put Your Network to Work

If you are successful in engaging your network of stakeholders, you will have a powerful resource to call upon for guidance, support and help.

Giving people a say in your plans and strategy will give them a sense of control. We tend to rebel when we feel we don't have control, so giving some, where it suits you, will reduce the likelihood of resistance in other areas.

Getting your stakeholders to physically help will be easier once they support you, but here are ten top tips to really galvanize them into Powerhouse action.

1. Ask when they are not busy, distracted or in a hurry.
2. Give them notice so they can schedule their help.
3. Be specific about what help you want, so it does not seem open-ended.
4. Give them clear instructions.
5. Make the first step easy.
6. Give them a deadline.
7. Let them know that others have already agreed to help.
8. Always give a reason why you need it – and ideally, why you chose them.
9. Act as if you expect them to say yes – people often comply with expectations.
10. Tell them what is in it for them if they help you.

... and finally, a free extra tip: look them in the eye and ask them clearly *'will you do this, by that date?'* Treat any response that is not a totally unambiguous 'yes' as a 'no', and find out what is holding them back from a 'yes'.

Relationships: 7 Powerhouse Pointers

1. Strategic networking is the process of transforming your relationships with the people around you into long-term assets.
2. To build a strategic network, you need to understand the power structure, attract people to you, create your reputation and build alliances.
3. When it comes to favours, it is better to give than to receive.
4. 'You can't build a reputation on what you are going to do.' Henry Ford.
5. For short-term stakeholders in your compelling causes, you need a simple, pragmatic and less strategic approach.
6. To engage with short-term stakeholders, you should identify and analyse the interested parties, plan and manage your campaign, then put your network to work.
7. Communication is not just about information: you need to win over hearts as well as minds.

5
Leadership
Get the Best From the People Around You

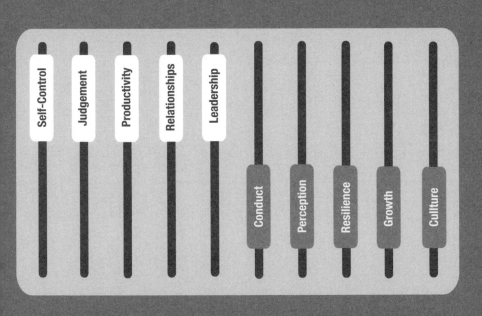

Self-Control

Judgement

Productivity

Relationships

Leadership

Conduct

Perception

Resilience

Growth

Culture

The true *Powerhouse* does not work alone. Having built relationships to support your work, you will also need to focus on immediate team members and colleagues who you can call on for practical assistance. How will you allocate work among them, secure guidance and support, and ensure people collaborate well and take responsibility for their portion of work? This chapter is about leadership, so I will also show you how to secure cooperation and ensure that people meet their commitments to you with their own Powerhouse capabilities.

Deploying Your Troops

**Powerhouse effectiveness comes most readily
when we play to our strengths.**

The fundamentals of managing and leading people are in giving each person the right role to play and the resources that they need to do it well. A Powerhouse knows that this does not happen by chance. Instead, you need to make careful decisions about how to assign work, you need to hand over the work properly, and you need to be able to monitor progress in a way that is transparent to everyone.

Assigning

When we do work we enjoy and work that we are good at, that work feels effortless. As we do it, we feel in control, we are aware of our progress and we have a calm, focused state of mind. Powerhouse effectiveness comes most readily when we play to our strengths; so when you assign work to other people, if you can, assign the work that they are drawn to.

A Powerhouse also knows that fairness is important to people. We worry less about what we are being asked to do and the rewards we are getting than we do about the person next to us. We want to know what our colleagues are up to. If we do, this makes it easier to collaborate, so make sure you communicate who is assigned to what work. When you give work to someone you have the opportunity to set them up to succeed, or possibly to fail.

There are five essential steps to a Powerhouse briefing, which you can remember easily as CODAC: Context, Outcome, Deadline, Authority and Commitment.

1. Context

Setting the context for the job serves several important functions, yet it is often something people miss out when briefing staff. It feels like irrelevant background so, when time is tight, it gets squeezed. However, context is vital. First, it gives the answer to the question why, and without that answer we tend not to be motivated. Second, taking the time to give some of the context shows trust and respect. Giving context will allow the other person to inject their own ideas and insights into their work. Finally, you don't want your own work constantly interrupted by a stream of unnecessary questions. The more thoroughly you brief at the outset, the less this will happen, and by giving a lot of background, people are better equipped to interpret the unexpected and make their own decisions.

2. Outcome

Think of this as your definition of success. If you are tasking me with a job, I will want to get good results – that's what will make me feel good about myself. So tell me what I need to aim for and how you will assess my work. The key Powerhouse concept here is of a Success Template: a specific set of things I need to achieve to make you entirely satisfied with my work. Once I have that, I can use it as my guide in what I am doing.

3. Deadline

Deadlines are vital so I can schedule my work effectively. For some people, the pressure of a deadline is also motivating.

4. Authority

If you ask me to do something, be clear with me how much authority you are giving me. This is at the heart of managing the risk of giving work to someone else, so if you have a high level of confidence that I will deliver, and the consequences of mistakes are constrained, then give me full authority. If, however, there are important consequences of errors and you don't have full confidence in my abilities, then make sure I can only take limited steps without checking back with you.

The three Rs of authority are: Rules, Resources and Reporting.

1. Rules: are there procedures, process, or steps I must follow? If so, let me know.
2. Resources: what resources can I access and is there an overall budget I must adhere to?
3. Reports: what reports do you need me to make?

5. Commitment

If it is a common mistake that managers skimp on the context, it is far more common and far, far more dangerous when they fail to secure a firm commitment from the person to whom they are delegating work. I guess that, once they have briefed, some managers just don't want to break the spell. They would rather just assume that all is well and leave it as an assumption that the other person will do as they are asked.

Always make sure that:

- Your instructions have been understood. 'What other questions do you have?' 'Are you completely clear about what I need?'

- The other person feels able to do the work. 'Are you able to do this piece of work?'
- The other person is committed to doing the work. 'Will you do this piece of work, by the date I set?'

Always treat any answer that is ambiguous or tentative as a 'no' and explore further. In return for this commitment, give your own commitment to provide the support and guidance that the other person needs.

Tracking

We need to see progress when we are working on something, because progress makes us feel good and seeing it gives us a sense that we are in control. You too need this information, to feel confident that the person working for you is on track. A Powerhouse loves progress.

The Japanese system of Kanban cards, used in just-in-time processing, provides a very simple and elegant way to display the progress of a range of jobs. To use it, you need to define generic stages that apply to the jobs. It doesn't matter if some jobs will not go through every stage, but it is important that each stage a job will go through is represented by one of your generic stages. Let's say the stages we want to use are: job identified, briefing, waiting to start, initial work, detailed work, quality check and signed off. Using these, we create a Kanban board – usually a chalkboard, a pin-board or a whiteboard, with these stages as seven columns. Now each new job gets its own Kanban card – a magnetic or sticky note, or a card, that can be placed onto the board. On each card write the name of the job, the deadline and the person to whom overall responsibility is assigned. Now place each card in the right column, as illustrated.

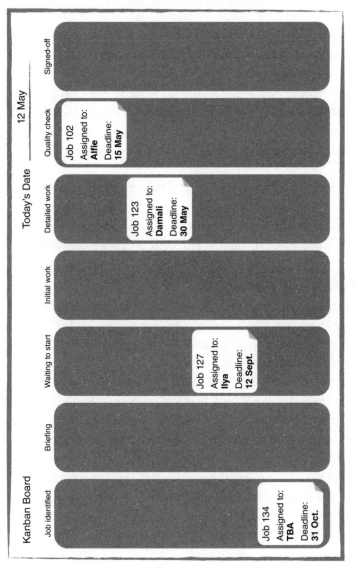

Kanban board

Winning Support

You get the team you deserve.

When you are planning work, the first task is to decide what you want to achieve, and why. Then you need to decide how you are going to do it. After that, you will think about how many people you require to help, what kind of people they should be, and what skills they will need. We have looked at all of this. Now you need to win their support by motivating them to deliver the Powerhouse performance you want.

You get the team you deserve. Not because the universe is fair: it isn't. But because if you work hard to engage, support and motivate your team, they will work hard to deliver the performance you want. If you don't do your bit: they won't do theirs.

Motivating Your Team

What motivates you? Almost certainly, it is lots of things. First, there are things like being safe, feeling secure, having a home and putting food on your table. These are the basic motivators that any job will address.

Then there are the things that lots of people think of, when asked this question: money, pleasures, rewards, toys, goods, holidays … These are the things that feel motivating. But, strangely, once we have a certain amount, having more of them makes very little real difference to our lives. We seem to know this instinctively, because their impact on our personal effectiveness, beyond showing up and doing what our contract says, is minimal most of the time. The exception is when you set your mind on one particular reward.

Powerhouse performance – from you and from the people you lead – comes from the small, subtle difference that four other motivators make. If you want to create Powerhouse performance, you need to give an extra GRAM of motivation.

GRAM stands for the four big motivators for Powerhouse performance:

1. Growth.
2. Relationships.
3. Autonomy.
4. Meaning.

1. Growth

We all need to feel that we are developing in our skills and knowledge and becoming more expert at the work we do. This is linked to our fundamental need for achievement, so you can motivate yourself and others by understanding the directions that each of us needs to grow in, and creating the opportunities to make real progress.

2. Relationships

For those who work full time, we spend more of our time awake with our work colleagues than we do with the people we deliberately choose to spend our lives with; partners and family. So good relationships at work are vital to our wellbeing. Some of us have a particularly strong need to be a part of a group, a family or a team. Attend to this by making team coherence a priority and building an environment of mutual care and support. You will always achieve more when you are prepared to forego the personal credit and rewards, and pass them on to the team of people who help you.

3. Autonomy

Relationships are important, but so is our need to feel in control of our lives and responsible for our own choices. For each of us, the balance between the needs for membership of groups and individual autonomy is different. You need to get to know the individuals who work for you, to find out where the right balance is for each of them. In some, this need for autonomy can manifest as a desire for authority and even power over others too.

4. Meaning

We all need to feel we have a purpose and we want that purpose to be worthwhile. Motivate by sharing the reasons for what your team are doing and strengthen it by giving each person the confidence that there is a plan that will achieve that purpose. People with the strongest need for autonomy, however, can easily find too much of a plan frustrating: it constrains their ability to feel in control of their lives. For them, provide an outline plan, focusing on middle and longer-term outcomes and leaving them more freedom to figure out how. For others, they will require greater certainty about the way they can achieve their outcome, so provide more detailed plans.

Communication is the Glue

What is it that holds a team together, mediates relationships and articulates meaning? A team is nothing unless communication works well at all levels: from the leader to team members, from the team members to their leader, and among team members. Teams need to share stories, resolve conflicts, solve problems and make decisions. All of these require that different people, with different knowledge and perceptions, are able to communicate effectively with one another.

The most fundamental Powerhouse communication skill is listening. Powerhouse listening means:

Focus on the other person and what they are saying:

- Don't judge what they say – just listen.
- Don't look for the next conversation – just listen.
- Don't try and figure out what to say next – just listen.

If you can train yourself to just listen, the quality of your understanding will improve, the quality of your questions will improve, and the quality of your relationships will improve.

The Psychology of Success

The leap from standard performance to Powerhouse performance is greater than the leap from under-performance to standard performance.

There is a new and exciting field of research that has grown up over the last 15 to 20 years, which is studying and learning from Powerhouse organizations that are really thriving. It is turning the lessons from these organizations into prescriptions for how to help your people and your organization flourish too. It is called Positive Organizational Psychology.

The transition from under-performance to standard performance often comes from a focus on three things: analysis of failures, feedback on shortcomings and enforcement of rules.

None of these, however, will leap your team to Powerhouse performance – which is arguably a greater leap than that from under-performance to standard performance. For that great leap, we need three new approaches to replace the more familiar list above: evaluation of excellence, celebrating success and constructive conduct.

Evaluate Excellence

A common managerial approach is to try to get to the root of failure, to dig it out and find alternative solutions. This works well when failure is the prevailing culture, but does not support good performers in achieving excellence. Instead, you need to focus

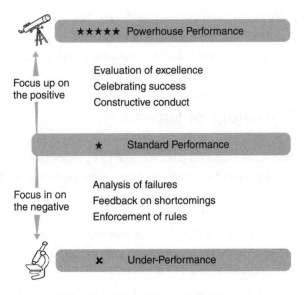

The leap to Powerhouse performance

on examples of excellence – the things that make a real positive difference – and understand them. Get your team together to learn from one another and encourage people to share success stories. Resilient salespeople understand that if they do not win, they need to learn from the experience. A Powerhouse knows that if they do win, they can learn from that experience.

Celebrate Success

Feedback on shortcomings often takes the form of criticism: 'you did well, but ...' For a Powerhouse performance:

cut the but.

Instead of a critical eye, learn to look for and celebrate examples of great performance. This works best when you do it often, as soon as you notice the valuable behaviours, and in a way that has meaning to the person whose great work you are noticing.

A fabulous resource is Diamond Feedback. Think of the four suits in a pack of playing cards:

- ♣ Clubs are for beating people up with.
- ♠ Spades are for digging down and finding out what went wrong, and why.
- ♥ Hearts are lovely, we use them to give unqualified, unspecific praise.
- ♦ Diamonds are valuable – use diamond feedback to focus on what I did and why it is valuable to you.

Behave Beneficially

It is easy to get into the habit of following the rules and treating your team members fairly. And this is good. For Powerhouse performance, though, you need to go further and treat people well. Do things wantonly that benefit the people around you, like offering gratitude, compliments and support. A few random acts of kindness to your team each week will have a huge impact on their performance.

One of the main things you can focus on is the relative frequency with which you respond positively to the things the people around you do or say. We often get into a mind-set of criticism, challenge and denial. To get the best out of people, aim to say three or more times as many positive things as you do negative things, throughout the day, in meetings and when working one-to-one with colleagues.

Securing Compliance and Completion

**The Jiminy Cricket effect is the way our
conscience holds us to account.**

Have you ever asked someone to do something and, a week later, they have not done it? Of course you have. What went wrong? The answer is often very simple: Jiminy Cricket was asleep on the job. Jiminy Cricket acts as Pinocchio's conscience. You and I have a Jiminy Cricket organ in our heads and, except in the few people out there with little integrity, it does a great job at reminding us to do what we promise ... as long as it was not asleep when we made the promise.

If you bump into a colleague, Jenny, in the corridor and ask for a favour, how often do you make a big deal of it? Probably, rarely. You don't want to because you don't want to draw attention to the fact that it is a favour and you feel uncomfortable asking for it.

So, when Jenny mumbles 'yeah, okay, leave it with me' you are delighted and move on quickly, before she changes her mind. The problem is: she wasn't paying a great deal of attention and so, when she mumbled her agreement, it wasn't a formal promise; she was just conforming to social convention.

Instead, you need to look Jenny in the eye and say: 'Have you got a moment?' and wait for her to respond.

When Jenny says 'yes', Jiminy is awake. If she says 'no', then she wouldn't have been able to commit properly anyway – so find out when she is free to talk.

Once you have Jenny's and Jiminy's full attention, you can ask for the favour. Now get a promise that Jiminy can enforce. Look Jenny in the eyes again and ask: 'Will you do that by Friday afternoon?' The deadline is important.

If she says yes clearly and confidently, then Jiminy will be on the job. Remind Jenny on Friday morning and, if she has not done it, her conscience will be pricked and Jiminy will be working hard to get it done.

If Jenny says no, then it is better to know that now, than to find out on Friday afternoon when she hasn't done it.

You can even test the strength of Jenny's promise. Ask what would get in the way of fulfilling it. If the answer is a solid reason why something specific could get in the way, then chances are that there is real concern to deliver on the promise. On the other hand, a lame reason like 'things might crop up' suggests instead that she is looking for excuses to not deliver.

Once you get a promise, acknowledge it by saying something like: 'Thank you for that commitment – it is important to me.' By adding the importance, of course, you are raising the stakes for her compliance.

Finally, don't feel shy about sending repeated reminders. Research by Paul Leonardi, Tsedal Neeley and Elizabeth Gerber found that managers who reminded team members about their assigned tasks multiple times and in different ways had considerably more success in gaining task completion on time.

So, to summarize:

1. Alert Jiminy Cricket that you are looking for a promise.
2. Set a deadline to trigger Jiminy.
3. Confirm that I have made a promise.
4. Tell me my promise is important.
5. Check the level of my commitment to my promise.
6. Remind me a few times along the way.

Leadership: 8 Powerhouse Pointers

1. Powerhouse effectiveness comes most readily when we play to our strengths.

2. Remember the five essential steps to a Powerhouse briefing as CODAC: Context, Outcome, Deadline, Authority and Commitment.

3. You get the team you deserve. Motivate your team through by using GRAM: Growth, Relationships, Autonomy and Meaning.

4. Communication is the glue that holds a team together.

5. The leap from a standard performance to a Powerhouse performance is greater than the leap from under-performance to standard performance.

6. For a Powerhouse performance: cut the but.

7. A few random acts of kindness to your team each week will have a huge impact on their performance.

8. The Jiminy Cricket effect is the way our conscience holds us to account.

6
Conduct
Get the Best From Yourself

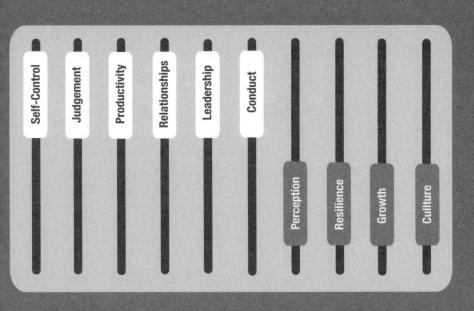

Powerhouse is a state of mind and a pattern of behaviour. Becoming this awesome source of effectiveness means transforming your thinking, your attitudes, your behaviours and, ultimately, becoming an inspiring leader.

Click, Bubble and Hum

Using the right thinking mode for each situation.

There are different ways that we all think. Each one is well tailored to different situations and being a Powerhouse means you are able to use the right thinking mode for each situation.

We will start with the three modes of thinking that get used most often at work; three modes I call: Click, Bubble and Hum.

Click: your fast responding, intuitive response is decisive and efficient.

Bubble: your logical, controlled thought processes give a rigorous response.

Hum: your reflexes and unconscious control of your body help you survive.

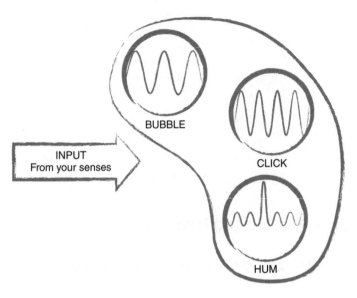

Click, Bubble and Hum

Click

Job Description: Efficiency

Click is your brain at its fastest and most efficient. Your brain in Click mode is on cruise, able to handle decisions quickly and with little thought, by accessing all of the rules that you have learned throughout the course of your life. When faced with a choice, Click leaps instantly into action and compares your situation with all of your past experiences and attempts to interpret the new in terms of the old, to develop a rapid response.

In many situations, this is not only efficient, but effective too. Click is your intuition at work. When your current situation is one that you have trained for, and for which your life experiences have prepared you well, Click will cut through all of the detailed information and focus on that which is most relevant. It will create a fast assessment of what is going on and what you should do next. Think of the Click mode as your gut instinct: you rarely know where it comes from, but it feels solid.

Problems arise when you are in a situation for which your past experiences have not prepared you completely. Click needs rules to use, but the rules you have are not quite right for the circumstances. In these cases, Click can let you down badly, making quick judgements that are wrong – sometimes disastrously so. Click has the ability to misread situations, fall into traps, and act on the wrong assessment.

These traps are one of the most important characteristics of the Click mode of thinking. To give it its speed and energy efficiency, Click acquires simple pathways that it likes to follow. Over millions of years of evolution, many such pathways – the thinking equivalent of downhill freeways – have evolved and are pretty much part of the way our brains develop through childhood into our adult state. While these patterns of thought may have served our ancestors well – and may continue to serve us well in certain situations – they represent easy judgements that are often wrong. They are biases in our thinking.

Five Biases of Click Thinking That Can Get You into Trouble

The First Thing Bias

Click latches onto the first information it receives and starts to compare everything to that. This means that the first speaker at a meeting, the first exam paper you mark, the first job application you review can all have a powerful effect on framing your assessment of a subsequent event.

The Whole Story Bias

Click does not like to work too hard. Consequently, it assumes that the information it has is all that there is. When it assumes it has the whole story, it makes judgements based on that, without bothering to check for missing evidence.

The Confirmation Bias

The first thing and the whole story biases are made worse still because Click will more easily notice information and events that confirm the assessment you have already made. This makes it hard to spot evidence that Click is wrong. The confirmation bias is responsible for the perpetuation of prejudices and so is, arguably, responsible for more ills in the world than any other single human factor.

The Familiar Story Bias

The Click mode likes to corral events into familiar patterns. It is good at reviewing your experience for stories of cause and effect, meaning, and correlation, and then finding a fit between current events and one of those stories. Where the fit is a genuine one, then Click has quickly solved its problem. However, where the fit is not precise, then any judgements Click makes are liable to be wrong.

The Recent Story Bias

Recent events make a greater impression on Click, making them more accessible for choosing what to do now. Consequently, where recent events are extraordinary and poorly represent what is likely to happen in the future, they can lead Click to make a decision that is unlikely to be right.

Click's job description may be efficiency, but efficient is not always effective. A Powerhouse needs more resources.

Bubble

Job Description: Rigour

Bubble is not efficient if we think in terms of energy usage and pace of thinking. The Bubble mode works slowly and uses a lot of energy to think through each situation with care. It is the conscious you that does the active thinking about events. Bubble allows you to build on ideas, assess risks and control events. The Bubble mode is analytical, logical and rigorous.

Use Bubble to examine situations that you don't understand, and to evaluate the rapid intuitive response that Click offers, before you act on it. Think of Bubble as Click's more responsible twin– when Click says: *'This is what to do!'* Bubble responds by saying: *'Let's think it through carefully first …'*

Click often jumps in when Bubble is not paying attention. When you attune your awareness to what is going on, you can sharpen your perception of details and distinctions that Click would miss. This is the strength of the Bubble mode: it has far more information to work from. It is also its weakness, because sometimes Bubble gathers too much information and can become overwhelmed by it. Paralysis by analysis is a symptom of your Bubble mode working too hard at a problem that simply needs Click's simplicity of reasoning.

Bubble thinking takes a lot of effort – literally. It uses a lot of energy and therefore can deplete your mental reserves. When you are engaged in careful Bubble thinking, you need to take breaks and refresh your brain with good food, fresh air and water. For most people, the morning is the best time to engage your Bubble mode, when you are rested and alert. By the end of the day, when you are tired, Bubble starts to give up.

Barack Obama knows how important it is to take the strain off Bubble. He has a very limited range of suit, shirt and tie styles, so that he can take anything out of the wardrobe and know that he will look good. By removing trivial decisions from Bubble's agenda, he can save energy for the big decisions that merit Bubble's full attention.

> *'You'll see I wear only gray or blue suits. I'm trying to pare down decisions. I don't want to make decisions about what I'm eating or wearing. You need to routinize yourself. You can't be going through the day distracted by trivia.'*
> Barack Obama, 44th President of the United States

Hum

Job Description: Survival Edge

Deep down in the most fundamental part of your brain lies Hum – the mode responsible for keeping you alive and reacting to threats. Hum offers automatic responses to basic stimuli. It is even faster and more efficient than Click, but its domain is limited to physiological responses to stimuli. Hum doesn't deliberate: it reacts. And its reactions trigger changes in our bodies and in the balance of hormones coursing through them. It has four default settings:

Setting 1: Alright

When everything is okay, Hum keeps our bodies ticking over as they should, and completely below the level of our consciousness most of the time. We breathe, we digest, our hearts beat, and our bodies maintain and mend themselves.

Setting 2: Fright

Hum responds to a shock or threat by closing everything down. We become frozen and unable to respond. This is Hum's way of stopping us stepping forward into danger. At times, however, in the modern world, Hum activates our fright setting at the wrong time, rendering us unable to proceed with important tasks.

Setting 3: Fight

Hum sometimes responds to a challenge by preparing for battle. This would be great if a wild animal were threatening your family, but when your boss takes you to task for producing a poor piece of work, or your client suggests that a competitor might do a better job, fighting is the last thing you need to do.

Setting 4: Flight

When Hum thinks it cannot win a fight, it tries to get us away from danger. Setting 2 turned everything off: Settings 3 and 4 turn back on the resources we need for fight or flight. In this case, your heart pounds, your muscles twitch, your mind races and you just want to get out of here. It is Hum that takes over when nerves start to get the better of you before an interview or presentation.

Hum is ever vigilant and that is its strength. It senses danger and prepares you to act. Its weakness is that it takes over so completely that Bubble often finds it hard to re-take control. But if you learn to spot the effects of Hum's intervention, and can mentally step back and relax, and then take a few deep, calming breaths to calm Hum's activity down, then Hum becomes the asset it should be, giving you a survival edge in troubled times.

Effectiveness = Efficiency + Rigour + Survival Edge

There are two other modes that most of us under-use. For full Powerhouse effectiveness, you need to be able to call upon Sigh mode and Squeak mode at the right times.

Sigh

Job Description: Insight

Sigh is your deep processing mode, which is often active in the background when little seems to be going on. Therefore, Sigh is the source of your creativity and your wisdom. You can think of Sigh as your 'unconscious consciousness' that is good at spotting the subtle, nearly imperceptible signs of change. Sigh is often your true decision-maker, but you need to be able to calm your mind to access Sigh's judgement and creative thinking.

You can access the awesome processing power of your Sigh mode through mindfulness, meditation and reflection. Taking time out of your busy day to consider, think, reflect and even to daydream, can give Sigh the time and space it needs to release the results of its deliberations into your conscious (Bubble mode) mind. This is why we often have creative thoughts first thing in the morning, eating breakfast, in the shower or bath, or walking. In these cases, Click often has nothing to respond to, Bubble is often relaxed, there are no threats for Hum to deal with. With Bubble quiet, it is able to hear the quiet voice of Sigh and bring it to your attention.

In Chapter 1, we saw the importance of making time to see around the next bend. This is the job of Sigh.

Squeak

Job Description: Empathy

Squeak is responsible for the short-term feelings that accompany human experience and affect the way we behave. It is your emotional response to events, to people and to your choices. Consequently, Squeak mode is vital in relationship building, in predicting and accommodating the needs of others and in maintaining your own equilibrium in tough times.

Squeak has a large palette of emotions to work with, from the primary colours of happiness, sadness, disgust, anger, fear and surprise, to more complex compounds, like love, jealousy, guilt, hope, contempt, trust and anticipation. Your ability to detect these in the people around you – called empathy – and to consider their implications for your choices adds a new dimension to your effectiveness when working in social, political and collaborative domains. The workplace is all of these, so Squeak is a vital mode to access.

Summary of the Five Modes

Mode	Job Description	Roles in Effectiveness
Click	Efficiency	Speed of response
		Access to intuition (deep learning)
		Decisiveness
Bubble	Rigour	Awareness of detail and subtlety
		Analysis and logic
		Control and consideration
Hum	Survival edge	Staying alive and healthy
		Regulating appetite, sleep and other requirements
		Reflexive response to threats
Sigh	Insight	Creativity
		Judgement
		Spotting signs – the next bend
Squeak	Empathy	Emotion
		Relationship building
		Resilience to pressure, adversity and stress

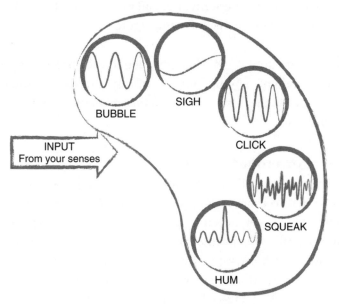

Click, Bubble, Hum, Sigh and Squeak

The Powerhouse Under Pressure

**A Powerhouse must understand the way our bodies
and minds respond to the pressures of stressful situations.**

Stress is not a bad thing. But the effects of stress can be devastating. Therefore, a Powerhouse must understand the way our bodies and minds respond to the pressures of stressful situations. When you do this, you can aim for the Powerhouse Peak.

For simple tasks, such as physical exercise or repetitive, administrative activities; the greater the level of mental and physical arousal, the higher our levels of performance. These tend to be the sort of jobs that need persistence, stamina or single-mindedness.

For more complex, mentally demanding work, too much arousal causes performance to decline, giving rise to a peak in productivity and performance, called the Powerhouse Peak. This is illustrated in the following figure.

The productivity zone lies between the complacency and low morale of tedium, and the anxiety and over-caution of pressure. At the centre of the productivity zone is the Powerhouse Peak.

The Powerhouse Peak

The Powerhouse Peak is characterized by highly focused attention. Here you are feeling fully capable of success and excellence, yet also stretched to the very limit of your experience and expertise. Work at the Powerhouse Peak demands your full attention and, consequently, you have constant awareness of how you are performing. Your perception is honed and you easily slip into flow states where time, discomforts and distractions

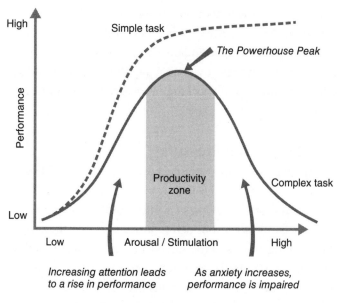

Powerhouse performance, under pressure

pass you by. These flow states not only offer peaks in productivity, creativity and clarity of thinking; they are also periods of intense satisfaction, that researcher and author Mihaly Csikszentmihalyi describes as optimal experiences. We experience subjectively high levels of contentment and pleasure.

The Stress of Boredom

Too little stimulation can be as stressful as too much. It also leads to under-performance where, at best, we accept okay as good enough and, at worst, we make mistakes or even create accidents. Too little stimulation can lead to depression.

A Powerhouse needs to take control and you can do this by deliberately putting yourself under pressure. Set demanding time limits that require astonishing speed and focus to achieve, or require exceptional levels of accuracy or quality. Decide to find ways to innovate that will bring improved value or faster completion times. Occupy your brain so that it does not have time to get bored. Turn mundane tasks, like filing or tidying up, into flow state activities by setting aggressive goals that stretch you to your limits and checking on progress constantly, to further tweak your performance.

Operating Under Pressure

In Chapter 8, we will examine how you can build the resilience to cope under pressure. A vital contributor to sustaining Powerhouse effectiveness is your ability to avoid choking under pressure. It can happen to all of us, from the weekend golfer making a mess of their drive on the eighteenth hole and losing the match, to the accomplished salesperson stumbling over their words at a critical sales presentation to a potential client.

How can a Powerhouse avoid choking under pressure? The simple answer is to ensure that what others would perceive as a high-pressure situation – like the ones above – are situations you perceive as ordinary. That is why the top professional golfers don't choke, and why the star salespeople make the perfect pitch even in the face of the biggest opportunities.

They constantly put themselves under pressure so that it becomes familiar and starts to seem ordinary. The more effectively you can simulate pressure in practice and rehearsals, and the more often you expose yourself to high-pressure situations, the more easily you will stay calm under pressure. So gradually increase the pressure you subject yourself to. In your mind, amplify the stakes for your next low pressure meeting, presentation or interview. This will prepare you for when the stakes are genuinely high.

Don't Be a Damn Fool

In the absence of an inspiring and worthy leader, people will follow any damn fool who sticks their head over the wall.

People want someone to follow. In the absence of an inspiring and worthy leader, they will follow any damn fool who sticks their head over the wall or steps forward. Don't be a damn fool. Be someone worth following. Be inspirational, be calm and centred, show integrity ... Be a worthy leader whom people will be inspired to follow.

Powerhouse is not about leadership; it is about effectiveness. But sometimes you need to lead to be effective. In these cases, what attitudes can you cultivate to be an effective leader and incite people to follow you, to support and challenge you and, crucially, to help you to make a difference? Here are the top ten Powerhouse attitudes.

Powerhouse Attitudes

Upright

Aim to be honourable, ethical and trustworthy. You need to be seen by the people you want to follow you as decent and fair, with a strong moral compass. The word integrity is overused. This one is old-fashioned but simple: you must be an upright member of your community.

Cool

Be calm under pressure, showing the great discipline and self-control that allow you to focus when others buckle: to triumph when others choke. And under pressure, a Powerhouse still expects the highest standards of themself and of others.

Pep

Pep means energy, vigour and self-confidence – almost the defining features of a Powerhouse. But it can also be an acronym, PEP, that stands for Passion, Energy and Poise, which together add up to the charisma, presence and impact that will draw people towards you and inspire them to follow.

Boldness

Have the courage to do what is right, and the confidence to have no regrets when you do. Boldness is about action more than words. While your words may inspire, it is your ability to follow through on your commitments that will cement your authority.

Heed

You can only be a true Powerhouse if you heed your environment and the people around you, paying attention to changes and pressures and acting in a courteous and respectful manner that is mindful of what matters in the long term.

Grit

If one thing will predict Powerhouse success more than any other, it is grit: the perseverance, the staying power and the stamina to stick with a compelling cause in the face of adversity. Grit is the passion and determination to keep going when others would quit. Without a doubt, this is also an appealing quality that leads people to follow.

Open

Be curious, imaginative and observant – open to experiences. But more than this, a Powerhouse leader needs to open themselves up to alternatives, wherever they come from, rather than being proud and didactic. This leads to the kind of adaptability that, when combined with grit, often gets results where others fail.

Hope

When things go badly, to whom do we look for inspiration and consolation? To the person we have chosen to follow. So the next Powerhouse attitude must encompass optimism, good cheer and buoyancy in the face of adversity. Hope may not be a strategy, but it transforms disappointment into determination.

Giving

An old fashioned view of leadership puts the leader at the top. But a Powerhouse leader knows that their role is to be generous with their time, their care and their praise. The concept of servant leadership is one where a Powerhouse sees their job as one of providing resources and protection to their team, to create an environment where the team can thrive and get Powerhouse results.

Thankful

One thing above all transforms leadership: gratitude for the team you have, rather than a constant focus on what you do not have, and how much better it would be if you had more, or better, or just different resources. Be thankful for what you have and look for ways to optimize the opportunities it offers.

Conduct: 10 Powerhouse Pointers

1. Click: your fast responding, intuitive response is decisive and efficient.
2. Bubble: your logical, controlled thought processes give a rigorous response.
3. Hum: your reflexes and unconscious control of your body help you survive.
4. Sigh: your slow-bake source of creativity, judgement and insight.

5. Squeak: your emotional response that builds relationships, feels and gives you resilience.
6. Effectiveness = Efficiency + Rigour + Survival Edge.
7. A Powerhouse must understand the way our bodies and minds respond to the pressures of stressful situations.
8. The Powerhouse Peak is where your productivity is at a maximum.
9. In the absence of an inspiring and worthy leader, people will follow any damn fool who sticks their head over the wall – don't be a fool: your people deserve better leadership than that.
10. Sometimes you need to lead to be effective: adopt the top ten Powerhouse attitudes.

7
Perception
Be Prepared for the Unexpected

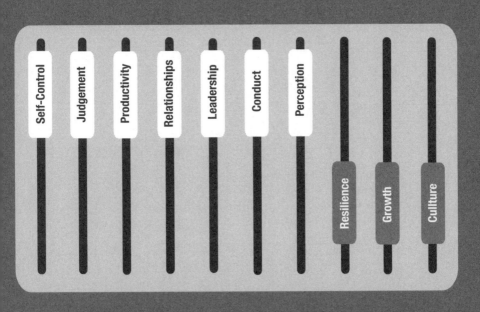

Self-Control
Judgement
Productivity
Relationships
Leadership
Conduct
Perception
Resilience
Growth
Cullture

A *Powerhouse* creates change, so the one thing you can be certain of is that things will sometimes go wrong ... but what things? It's time to foresee trends and changes, understand people, assess the risks and figure out how to deal with them in a pragmatic and efficient manner.

Reading People

The secret of reading people's moods and intentions is simple: pay attention. The signs are usually there for you to notice.

What matters is patterns; so to understand a person, you need to build up a mental model of how they behave over time. When you use this careful observation to assess whether their behaviour now is consistent or not, you can often tell what they might do and how they may respond.

Ask yourself five questions:

1. *What do they want?*
   This will help you figure out how to motivate people.
2. *What do they think?*
   This will help you to get an insight into people's thoughts.
3. *What will they do?*
   This will give you an idea of what choice they will make.
4. *How will they decide?*
   This will help you to influence the choices they make more effectively.
5. *How will they act?*
   This will help you to anticipate their approach and work together more effectively.

You will never be able to achieve certainty and complete accuracy; people are far too complex for that. But by being observant and noticing things, and combining that with a simple understanding of how to interpret some of the signs, you will achieve a far greater ability to decode the signs and predict behaviour.

What Do They Want?

The answer to this question will be driven by what the person cares about and, in the workplace, there are four common answers to this question. When you get to know someone, you can use your understanding of which of the drivers is strongest to help motivate them, by framing what you need them to do in terms of what they care most about.

Authority

Some people care about status and power. They need to feel both the social aspects of their authority and a sense of control. For people like this, emphasize how the work you are giving them offers a chance to make their own choices, and that doing it well will contribute to raising their status. It is when this goes to extremes that we recognize people throwing their weight around and acting like dictators. They become driven less by the desire to gain authority, and more by the fear of losing what they have.

Popularity

For some people, relationships and feeling part of a group are the most important aspects of what they do. They like to feel needed and included, and they get pleasure from participating in a social structure. Show them how the work you are giving them offers the chance to collaborate with others and strengthen their social bonds. At extremes we sometimes see people so motivated by the need to be popular that they will defend it at whatever cost, adopting a martyr mentality and taking on anything they are asked to do, rather than risk offending by saying no.

Achievement

We all like to see progress, but this is what really drives some people. For them, each success adds to their esteem and provides external validation. They like to increase their skills and expertise, and to feel that these are highly valued. Show them how the work you are setting them will be hard but achievable, to increase the promise of successful achievement. There are two ways that extremes of a strong drive towards achievement can go wrong: either an extreme aversion to any kind of risk, driven by a fear of failure, or alternatively, a cowboy mentality of taking short-cuts and even risks to achieve something when under excessive pressure.

Significance

For some people it is the meaning and purpose of what they are doing that matters most. They need to feel that there is a good reason for it and that this will make it – and them – significant. Show them why you are asking them to do the work you need, and show how their effort will make a real contribution to something that matters. The need for everything to have meaning can, at extremes, lead to a highly judgemental attitude that challenges everything and in which little or nothing seems to this person to be sufficiently worthwhile to fully engage them.

What Do They Think?

When people speak, they may expose their true thoughts or not:

- They may be open and plain to see.
- They may be disguised. What is on show is a mask ... a lie.
- They may be hidden from others, or closely guarded.
- They may be unfound: yet to be decided upon.

The secret to reading whether someone's thoughts are their true thoughts (open) or disguised (a lie) lies in the consistency of their behaviour: their congruence or incongruence. And if you cannot read their thoughts, how can you know whether they have yet to make up their mind, or they know and are hiding it? It is the same thing: congruence and incongruence. For this, you need to start by establishing a baseline of normal, un-threatened behaviour.

Baselining

Nothing beats observing someone over time to get a good idea of their normal behaviour and how they respond to events. The better you know someone, the more easily you will be able to spot behaviour that is out of the ordinary and may, therefore, signal incongruence.

Sometimes, however, you don't have this luxury. Negotiators often start off a negotiation with a period of rapport building. For experts, this is not just about building a relationship because negotiating is a social activity. They are watching carefully, trying to gauge a pattern of normal responses before the stresses of the negotiation proper start up. Simple questions like 'have you had a good weekend?' will give you a sense of how people act when they answer a question without any need to dissemble.

Observing

Once you have a baseline, ask direct questions, and then listen carefully to the answer and the way that they give it. Avoid saying too much or giving options for the other person to do anything other than answer the question you have posed. Just be quiet and listen for clues. This way, they have to do the work and you will get the maximum amount of information from them.

Signs of Incongruence

Incongruence means that some aspects of what they are saying fail to match others. Often, body language, gestures, expressions or tone of voice do not fully reflect what they are saying. The simplest clues to spot are signs of stress or evasion.

Signs of stress include touching or playing with their neck, collar, tie or necklace, rubbing their thighs (a common stress relief gesture), or tightening of facial, neck or upper body muscles. You may notice them clench their teeth, compress their lips or furrow their brow, for example. The problem is that these stress signals can also indicate a more general anxiety, which may arise from the perceived pressure of the situation rather than from a concern about being deceitful. Another set of muscles that we clench when stressed are the throat muscles, leading to raised pitch and uneven vocal tone. These are what we hear from a nervous speaker, for example.

Signs of evasion include looking away, longer than usual blinks, covering up the mouth or even the eyes, and stalling before answering, for example by clearing the throat or taking a glass of water. When people are confident with what they are saying, they speak fluently with minimal hesitation and tag phrases, such as 'you know', 'sort of' or 'ums and ers'. More of these than is usual (the baseline state) can indicate evasion or deceit. There are no absolute rules, but usually, when people add phrases like 'I'm sure', it is themselves they are trying to convince, not you. 'I'm sure' often means they are not.

Perhaps the greatest clues are those that seem not to signal deceit. Everyone knows that liars avoid your gaze, so if someone is holding eye contact more than usual, ask yourself why. Likewise, we naturally fidget when we feel uncomfortable, so if someone seems unnaturally stiff and still, they may be trying to suppress the fidget. Look out for clamped hands and an overly rigid posture that indicate an attempt to over-control movement. This is true in language too. When people are lying to you, they will often try harder to control their language, making less use than usual of common contractions like can't, I'm or won't. More use than usual of cannot, I am and will not can all be tell-tale signs

What Will They Do?

Knowing what someone wants and what they are thinking can give you a strong indication of what they might do. And once again, knowing someone well will help you to predict what choice they will make. In this case, it helps to know what drives their choices. Whilst most of us balance a number of different priorities when we decide what to do, we each have a favourite, and if you know what their default preference is, you can start to analyse how much it will apply to a particular situation.

Four common preferences are:

- *'I want it quickly'* means I will prefer an option that offers speed.
  The danger for such people is that more haste can mean less speed, and that by rushing they will make mistakes.
- *'I want the best'* means I will prioritize quality over other factors.
  The danger for such people is that they are never satisfied and find it hard to finish their work.
- *'I don't want to pay too much'* means I will prefer a low-cost option.
  The danger for such people is that a focus on cost can mean they lose sight of value.
- *'I don't want to get it wrong'* means I will go for the safe option.
  The danger for such people is that the safe option may not be the right option.

How Will They Decide?

Different people have different ways to come to their decisions. Five common types can each be influenced using different strategies.

Eureka

What they will say: 'Is this a great idea?'

Eureka deciders can be entranced by new ideas and will only take the trouble to evaluate them once they have become excited by them. Their evaluation, however, tends to be rigorous, because they need to satisfy themselves that the idea is truly a good one and will justify the risks involved as they tend to be risk takers, looking for a higher return on their efforts and investments.

Persuade them in stages, focusing first on the big picture, then on results, and finally on the details of risk, return and management. A danger to be aware of is that the Eureka decider finds an idea too boring and will fail to act.

Logic

What they will say: 'Does this make sense?'

Logical deciders will pull apart every last detail of a proposition before making up their mind. They need time to think it through, and you will need to satisfy them that you have missed nothing in assessing implications, complications and risks; they really don't like surprises.

Persuade them with facts, data, research and analysis, from as many independent sources as possible. Set out your methodology clearly and then sit back and let them take as much time, and ask as many questions, as they need. Rushing them will be a big mistake. A danger to be aware of is that the Logical decider will not find your arguments rigorous enough and will fail to act.

Safety in Numbers

What they will say: 'Is this tried and trusted?'

Safety deciders want to know that they won't be trying something new and risky. If a proposal is new to them, they will look to their trusted colleagues to advise them, and if they have none with sufficient experience, they will need case studies, real world experiences and testimonials to make the case. More than any others, Safety deciders will often default to a leading brand in a purchasing decision, or an established procedure to get things done.

Persuade them with proofs, testimonials and explanations that will make your proposal seem more familiar. You need to make them feel that their decision is one that any reasonable person would take. A danger to be aware of is that the Safety decider will not feel safe enough and will fail to act.

Gut Instinct

What they will say: 'Can I trust you?'

Gut deciders want to trust their intuition and, if they don't have the experience to assess your proposal in this way, their default will be to assess you instead. So they will challenge you – not just to test the evidence, but also to see how you respond. What they want is to fit you and your evidence into their established model of the world. This means they can seem aggressive and contrary, but once they trust you and get hooked on your proposal, they will go all-in on taking over the idea and the risks involved.

Persuade them by establishing your credibility from the outset, and then the credibility of your proposals. Relate everything to their own experiences, background and preferences, and don't be too proud to use a little intellectual flattery. Two dangers to be aware of are that the Gut decider will either not trust their instinct and will fail to act, or will be let down by their intuition and will choose poorly.

My Way

What they will say: 'I know my own mind.'

As their name suggests, My Way deciders are pretty hard to persuade, because they always want to do things their own way, adopting their own ideas. Indeed, you need to be very careful not to get caught trying to manipulate them, because if they sense that their idea was really your idea, then they will put you straight to the front of the queue for blame if anything goes wrong. My Ways tend to be even more domineering than Gut deciders and will often focus in on small details that they understand to avoid exposing personal weaknesses. They don't like to listen, they do jump to conclusions, and they will look for ways to avoid responsibility when they can.

Don't try to persuade them. Give up any desire for credit (because blame is its evil flip-side) and be prepared for a long process of presenting evidence that will allow the My Way decider to form their own conclusion. Clear structured arguments are essential, but do not let them stray into advocacy. A danger to be aware of is that the My Way decider will fail to act on an essential idea, just because it was not *their* essential idea.

How Will They Act?

The way people act follows patterns that they have evolved over a lifetime of social interactions. Once you get to know them, you can recognize their style and therefore some of the ways that they will go about fulfilling a task. The four basic approaches are:

Butterflies: 'Let's All Get on With it'

Energetic, creative and sociable butterflies like working as a team and seeing visible progress. If they don't get that, they get bored instead. This makes them workplace butterflies – always attracted to the brightest flowers around. But when they are on your team and fully engaged, you can count on enthusiasm and collaboration from butterflies. Their strong social instincts, combined with their desire for progress, create a big weakness in butterflies: if they are not seeing the results they want, they can stoop to manipulating people to get them.

Bunnies: 'Let's All Get on'

Harmony is more important than progress to a bunny, who will do anything to avoid confrontation. But their strength lies in their desire to keep the team together, cooperating loyally to the very end. You can count on them to work hard to maintain team morale, but you will need to go to someone else when you want to drive the team harder. The problem bunnies sometimes create is a lack of progress, with an over-focus on social processes.

Beavers: 'Let's Do it Properly'

Beavers work hard – often alone – to make sure the team gets things just right. They are acutely aware of the risks of failure and are never happier than when they are going over the details one more time. Beavers are extremely reliable, but they will demand plans and predictability, so if those are not in place, expect the Beaver to stop and work on creating them. You may therefore need to move them on, because a beaver can spend too much time polishing a stone that is shiny enough.

Sharks: 'Let's Just Do it'

Let's get on and get it done. And we'll do it my way. The shark is forceful and task focused, with little concern for the feelings that matter so much to bunnies. If they don't see progress, a shark will quickly get frustrated, and don't expect much tolerance of failure: sharks can leave a trail of blood in the water, marking their last dinner.

Seeing Around Corners

The world of work is like playing chess: being successful means being several moves ahead.

For a Powerhouse, the world of work is like playing chess: being successful means being several moves ahead. In many sports the advice is the same, whether it is tennis, football or ice hockey; in the words of Wayne Gretzky's father Walter, his first coach:

'Skate where the puck's going,
not where it's been.'

Never assume that your plan will work – all it is, is your best estimate of what will happen if things go the way you expect and everybody does what you ask of them. Anticipate problems. This is the principle of *sensen no sen*.

Sensen No Sen

In traditional Japanese martial arts, the ultimate goal is to use minimal force and effort to control an adversary. If you have to compete, you will be making life difficult. Techniques can be practiced at three levels of increasing sophistication and subtlety.

Go no sen represents a defensive counter move that responds to an attack. What is happening is clearly visible, so your task is to quickly select a suitable way to deal with your attacker's power. Before the actual attack is visible, your attacker will be physically committed to their attacking move and the more sophisticated student can anticipate the attack and blend with it simultaneously. This is called *sen no sen*. The most skilled practitioners can read the attack even earlier, at the point their attacker becomes psychologically committed to attacking, but possibly before their body knows how they will attack. Sensing the intent allows the practitioner to pre-empt the attack and deal with it with minimum effort and maximum control. This is *sensen no sen*. It is why a Powerhouse needs to spend time peering around the next bend

Opportunities

Too much focus can create tunnel vision. This is the danger that arises when we become complacent about our successes. There can be a big opportunity – or threat – around the next bend, but we don't spot it because we are too busy looking forward.

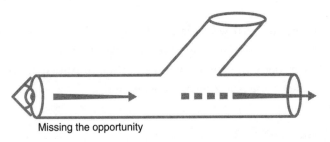

Missing the opportunity

Missed opportunity

A Powerhouse can find it easy to spot opportunities early by keeping constantly alert for them.

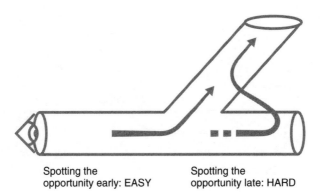

Spotting the
opportunity early: EASY

Spotting the
opportunity late: HARD

Spotting opportunities early

But, as always, a Powerhouse should be looking for a better way; not just being alert, but actively looking for opportunities.

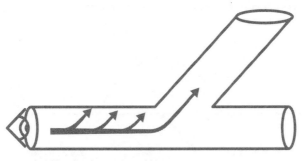

Looking for the opportunities

Constantly looking for opportunities

If you maintain this approach, and keep honing your perception, you will eventually be able to spot the faintest glimmer of a sign that will allow you to attain *sensen no sen* abilities. This means accessing the deep processing mode of thought called Sigh, which we met in the last chapter.

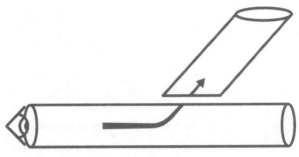

Sensen no sen
Sensing the opportunity before others can spot it

Sensen no sen

Horizon Scanning

Do you remember the idea of a meerkat surveying the horizon, to identify any changes that you need to think about? That was in Chapter 1. Now it is time to look at a simple three-step Powerhouse process for scanning your horizon.

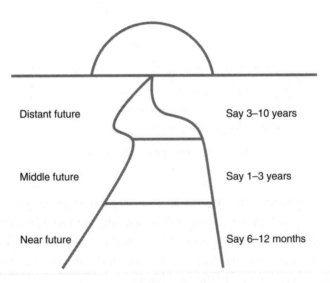

Horizon scan

Step 1: Trends

Look out for the trends, changes, patterns and plans that can affect your future. For example, this could mean social, economic, technological or environmental trends and pressures. Record the impacts of each into three time windows: the near future, the middle future and the distant future. Your context will determine how long each of these periods will be for you, but as a typical guide, you might expect:

- Near future: six to twelve months.
- Middle future: one to three years.
- Distant future: three to ten years.

How can you spot these trends? Here is a simple mnemonic, SPECTRES, that will help you remember eight typical sources; the spectres of the future.

1. *Social* trends and pressures.
2. *Political* and fashion changes.
3. *Economic* forces and trends.
4. *Commercial* pressures and changes.
5. *Technological* trends and fashions.
6. *Regulatory* constraints and changes.
7. *Environmental* pressures and imperatives.
8. *Security* needs and constraints.

Step 2: Knock on Effects

Starting with the near term, for each time period, look at the pressures and changes you have identified, and ask yourself what they mean for the following period?

Then start again at the far term and for each period ask what do the pressures and changes you have identified mean for the preceding period?

Step 3: Opportunities and Threats

From this analysis, identify the significant opportunities for you and your organization. Consider the value, complexity, scale and sustainability of each of them to determine those with the highest priority to you and your organization. Now do the same for the threats. Prioritize them by considering the impact, the likelihood and the proximity of each one.

Spotting Risks

> *'Bad luck doesn't exist. There is only what we couldn't know or what we hadn't been able to foresee.'*
> Enzo Ferrari, a Powerhouse if ever there was one

There are two types of risk, and the first is the 'hidden future' – the gaps in our knowledge, the things we couldn't know. These are the catastrophes, breakdowns and disruptive new entrants into our markets. We can start to deal with these risks with research, exploration, data gathering and horizon scanning. We can tempt fate in a controlled way with tests, pilots and prototypes. These allow us to understand and predict some risks, and convert what remains into irreducible risks that are purely statistical: 'casino risks'.

Casino risks are those we know about and understand. But for all of our understanding, prediction is impossible. We know precisely the likelihood of 24 black coming up, but we will never predict which spins of the wheel will give that result. A lot of weather problems and manufacturing errors are like this. We cannot reduce the risks to zero, but with better statistical data, we can improve our forecasting, prioritize better and make intelligent judgements about what contingencies to allow.

Step 1: Spot the Risks

Spot = Identify + Analyse

Identify: What Could Go Wrong?

The first thing we do is think through our activities from the perspective that something will go wrong: there will be some failure, some mistake or some hazard. The SPECTRES of failure are everywhere, so use the same acronym that we met in the previous section to identify the threats to your activities.

Analyse: How Bad is it?

For each risk, assign it a score based on how bad it would be, and how likely you think it is to happen. This will allow you to prioritize your risks. A Powerhouse knows the value of simplicity, so please do not over-complicate this process for fear of letting the precision of your estimates blind you to what matters. For most projects that you will take on, estimating risk is an inexact process; it is your judgement about how to handle a threat that matters.

So, for an office move, you might consider a two-day disruption in IT services as awkward and highly likely, whilst the new building not being completed and safe to enter would be serious but low likelihood in the context of progress to date.

	Low Likelihood Little need for concern	**Medium Likelihood** Could well happen	**High Likelihood** Seems to happen a lot
Disastrous Impact Project failure	Amber	Red	Red
Terrible Impact Contingency blown / All objectives missed	Amber	Amber	Red
Serious Impact Rethink plans / Use significant contingency	Green	Amber	Red
Awkward Impact Problems need fixing / Use of contingency	White	Amber	Amber
Minor Impact Fix on the run / Contingency not needed	White	Green	Amber

Risk analysis

KEY:

Red Basket of management strategies needed	**Amber** Management plan needed	**Green** Monitor the risk for changes in profile	**White** No action needed

Step 2: Handle the Risks

Handle = Plan + Action

Plan: What Can I Do About it?

There are six distinct risk management strategies, from which you can develop your specific plans.

1. **Avoid it**: change your plans, so that you do not incur the risk.
2. **Preventative measures**: take steps to make the risk less likely to occur.
3. **Mitigate the effects**: design actions that will make the impact less severe, if the risk materializes.
4. **Plan B**: create a contingency plan, so you know what to do if the risk occurs.
5. **Get someone else to carry the can**: transfer the risk to someone better able to minimize it or deal with it. Contracting with experts does the former, while insurance does the latter.
6. **Do nothing**: if the risk is not serious enough and if none of the strategies above offer good value for the time and resources you would need to invest, then do nothing and accept that the risk may occur.

Action: Take Action

Once you have a plan, then put it into action. If this process is sounding familiar ... it should. These are the four steps in the Powerhouse Loop. So you know what to do next: identify if any new risks have emerged, re-analyse all outstanding risks, review your plans, and take further action.

Perception: 6 Powerhouse Pointers

1. The secret of reading people's moods and intentions is simple: pay attention. The signs are usually there for you to notice.

2. Ask yourself five questions to help anticipate the behaviour of others: What do they want? What do they think? What will they do? How will they decide? How will they act?

3. The world of work is like playing chess: being successful means being several moves ahead.

4. There can be a big opportunity – or threat – around the next bend, but we don't spot it because we are too busy looking forward.

5. *Sensen no sen*: sensing intent allows you to pre-empt an attack and deal with it with minimum effort and maximum control.

6. *'Bad luck doesn't exist. There is only what we couldn't know or what we hadn't been able to foresee.'* Enzo Ferrari.

8
Resilience
Handle the Unexpected

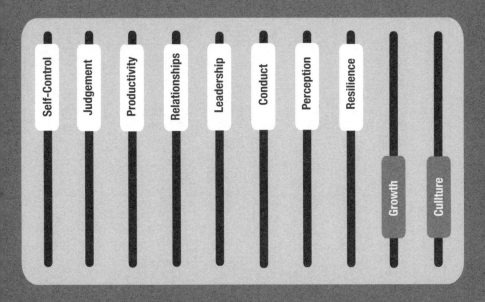

A *Powerhouse* needs to stay in control when things are changing at their fastest. You will be at the heart of constant change, so how can you deal with shift effectively and respond to problems?

Intelligent Perseverance

... or why a retired USAF Colonel has the secret to personal, professional and corporate success

A Powerhouse will sometimes fail. That is the price for going to the cutting edge of effectiveness. What matters is how you handle it. Admit it, understand it, figure out its causes and create procedures to prevent it from happening again. You need to constantly refine how you do things to create consistent, effective processes.

You need to persevere, but intelligently. If you simply keep doing what you have been doing, you will keep getting what you have been getting. In the face of adversity and constant change, you need to adapt continually to your new circumstances, and find new ways to achieve the outcomes to your compelling causes.

The OODA Loop

One man who knew all about this was Colonel John Boyd. As a US Air Force pilot, he saw action as a fighter pilot in the Korean War and went on to teach at the prestigious USAF Fighter

Weapons School. It was there that he started to develop his ideas of manoeuvrability, which eventually crystallized into his concept of a decision cycle. Boyd argued that, as we cope with a constantly changing environment, we must constantly re-evaluate what is happening and decide what to do next. As a skilled fighter pilot, he went on to assert that by going around that decision cycle faster than an opposing pilot, he could gain rapid air superiority. Certainly his performance as a pilot seemed to bear that out.

As a military theorist, he went on to give this cycle a name: the OODA Loop. OODA stands for the four components of the cycle:

1. Observe – identify what is happening
2. Orient – analyse what it means
3. Decide – make a plan for your next step
4. Act – take action.

The OODA Loop is just the flip-side of the Powerhouse Loop.

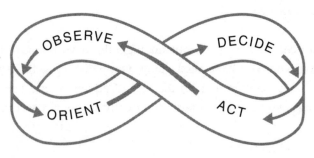

The OODA Loop

Making Boyd's OODA Loop work for you requires qualities that we have already seen. Of the ten Powerhouse attitudes that we examined in Chapter 6, four of them translate directly onto the stages of the OODA Loop.

Observe – Heed

You first need to heed your environment and the people around you, soaking up a thorough understanding of what has changed. The whole of Chapter 7 should have helped to prepare you for this. It is about the Power Switch of Perception.

Orient – Open

A Powerhouse needs to be open to a host of influences and interpretations if they want to adapt effectively to any circumstances. Boyd described this step as the heart of the OODA Loop. This is where you analyse and synthesize information from a host of sources. Boyd specifically described four:

- Your genetic heritage.
- Your cultural traditions.
- Your previous experiences.
- New information.

He argued that without the full context of your background, you cannot create a robust analysis of your present situation. This relates very well to the Power Switch that is described in the next chapter: Growth.

Decide – Cool

A Powerhouse has to be cool and calm under pressure, showing the great discipline and self-control that allows one to focus on what the options are, and which is the best course of action. For fighter pilots like Boyd, this is where the manoeuvrability matters – how quickly can you change direction? The tools you need for this are mostly in Chapter 2, where we looked at the Power Switch: Judgement.

Act – Grit

Grit is the perseverance, the staying power and the stamina to stick with a compelling cause in the face of adversity. Grit is the passion and determination to keep going when others would quit. Act with total commitment to your decision, and observe the outcome of your choice. This is largely about conduct, the Power Switch we looked at in Chapter 6.

Perception, Judgement, Adaptability and Perseverance

Perseverance means going around in a circle, until the job is done. But while perseverance alone may create a kind of productivity, it is not enough for Powerhouse effectiveness. You need intelligent perseverance. Don't just 'stick to the plan' in the face of setbacks and change: adapt yourself and your approach to the new circumstances.

Intelligent Perseverance = Perception + Judgement + Adaptability + Perseverance

A Powerhouse need to focus on the vital few things that will make the most difference. This is what will create Powerhouse effectiveness. It may seem safer to do a bit of everything, but that would lead you to excellence at nothing. But focus is risky: what are you not looking at?

This is why you need to keep everything else in your peripheral vision, constantly looking for opportunities or threats – as we saw in the last chapter. Effectiveness is not about certainty: it is about committing to what is right and adapting to changes in circumstances. That is intelligent perseverance.

Shovelling the Shift

When shift happens, Powerhouse effectiveness means being able to deal with all the problems that arise, effectively and efficiently.

Shift happens and things go wrong. When this happens, Powerhouse effectiveness requires an ability to deal with all the problems that arise, effectively and efficiently. This means being able to rein-in your Hum response and fully engage your Bubble.

Sponts and Ords

How do you respond to changes in circumstances? Some people embrace whatever comes along. They enjoy adapting themselves to new situations and actively prefer to keep as many options open as possible. Surprises enchant them, so they tend not to like planning, preferring the flexibility to respond to whatever comes along. They tend to be adaptable, spontaneous and sometimes even impulsive. Others prefer their lives to be predictable, so that they know what they can expect. Decisions close off options and that makes them feel more comfortable, because they dislike uncertainty. Surprises and sudden change unsettle them and it takes time for them to regain their equilibrium and figure out what next. They tend to be organized, orderly and sometimes even controlling.

So, do you see yourself as more of a spontaneous Spont or an orderly Ord?

Not surprisingly, a Powerhouse needs to access the strengths of both Sponts and Ords. Whichever you are, you need to learn the skills to create balance: Sponts learning the discipline of planning and preparation (Chapter 3), and Ords honing their situational awareness (Chapter 7) and learning the skills to adapt to change, in this chapter.

Suppress Hum

Sponts and Ords can both suffer from the same problem: sudden change can trigger emotional and reflexive responses from your Hum mode, leading to an inability to accurately assess the situation. Once your physiological responses settle down, Click kicks in. In Sponts, Click says: 'Yay – time to play' and grasps the first opportunity it sees, not bothering to assess whether there are better opportunities available, nor evaluating the risks involved. In Ords, Click says: 'Oh – time to go'. It looks for the best way to ignore what has happened and get on with what it was doing. It misses the new opportunities and can even ignore the new threats.

The Hum mode leads inevitably to a Click decision. A Powerhouse needs to suppress Hum and engage Bubble. This will allow you to identify the shift, analyse the shift, and plan how you will respond to the shift: the Powerhouse Loop.

The way to engage Bubble is to immediately respond with the SCOPE process. This is a five-step Bubble response to anything unexpected.

1. **Stop**: physically and mentally take a step back; a long enough pause to let your Bubble mode engage. A few deep breaths can really help at this stage.
2. **Clarify**: deliberately observe what has happened. Ask yourself questions and seek out the answers. Gather the information you need to make an informed choice. This mental control forces your mind to lock into Bubble mode.
3. **Options**: now consider your options for how to proceed. What are your choices, what are the risks and merits of each one and, consequently, which one will you choose?
4. **Proceed**: now it is time to take action. Commit yourself to your choice of options and focus on making that work. This focus will suppress any emotion or panic that might trigger a re-emergence of Hum mode.
5. **Evaluate**: by now, you understand the essential nature of the Powerhouse Loop. It is a loop. So constantly monitor the effectiveness of your actions and evaluate the impact they are having. Where necessary: stop …

Powerhouse Modes in Times of Shift

Each situation demands a different response. But there are six ways you can tackle a situation, depending on its nature and what the priorities are.

Leader Mode – for When People are Scared

Use leader mode when you need to take charge and inspire confidence in the people around you. Take control and make decisive decisions, but also show that you are prepared to share the consequences: the risks, the discomfort and the workload that is entailed. Now is the time to review what we learned about motivation in Chapter 5.

Exploration Mode – for When the Situation is Unclear

Adopt exploration mode when you need more information to form a robust decision, or design a solution to the problem at hand. Investigate, gather data, and conduct tests or experiments. Your role here is to stabilize the situation and then apply maximum brain-power to understanding what is going on.

Process Mode – for When it Helps to Do it by the Book

Some tricky situations need you to focus on systems and procedures, to reduce the risks of error under pressure, to instil confidence with the reassurance of routine, and to reduce the cognitive load that decision-making requires, so that you can free up your mental horsepower for other things.

Fix-it Mode – for When You Know the Problem

Go into fix-it mode when the problem is clear and what you need is a solution. Reliable problem solving needs a clear understanding of the problem, so if you don't have this, return to exploration mode.

Crisis Mode – for When There is Real Danger

When an emergency response is needed, go into crisis mode. Become authoritarian and direct activities clearly and precisely. Focus on only what needs to be done to make everything safe and secure, and set everything else aside.

Supporting Mode – for When Others Know What to Do

There will also be times when you can do nothing practical to progress the situation. What you need to do is to support the people involved in what they need to do. Supporting mode is caring and compassionate towards the people affected by, or dealing with, the implications of the shift. Offer personal attention, but remain mindful of the risks of over-committing yourself. The third major section of this chapter, Weebling, will deal with this aspect of shift.

Say No by Saying Yes

Of course, you won't always be working on your own compelling causes: sometimes you will be carrying out projects for other people; maybe other organizations. What do you do when you receive a request to change what you are doing? Not surprisingly, the answer is based on the Powerhouse Loop again.

We start the loop with a shift in requirements. You may be tempted to say: *'Yes, bring it on. Let's just do it!'* But this could be foolish: what if the person requesting the change is wrong and there is little benefit or much risk? Maybe you should say *'NO, we made a good decision, let's stick with it!'* This too could be foolish: what if there is a compelling need for this change, or there are substantial benefits to be gained?

Instead, analyse the request. Compare the reasons for the request and the benefits of the change, against the costs, the resources needed, the delays that would be incurred and

$$Q = P_1 + P_2 + P_3 + P_4$$

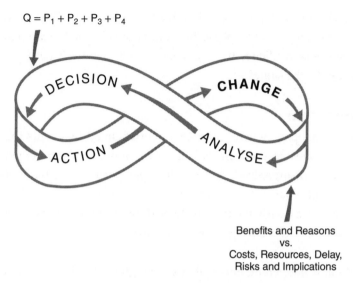

Benefits and Reasons
vs.
Costs, Resources, Delay,
Risks and Implications

The shift loop

the risks involved. Use this analysis as a basis for a decision. Remember back to the algebra of decision-making in Chapter 2:

Decision Quality = Proof + Process + Perspective + Protection

By saying yes to the request, you have a mechanism to say yes or no to the shift. Now take action and implement the decision.

This creates a structured and accountable response to shift. Make sure that you also keep good records of what was requested, who requested it, your analysis and the decision that was taken. Then inform the people who need to know.

Weebling

> *'Weebles wobble ... but they don't fall down.'*
> Advertising slogan, used by Hasbro Playskool

Weebles were a popular children's toy in the 1970s. They were built so they would wobble, but could not fall over: the ultimate symbol of resilience to hard knocks. How would it be if you could be the same?

Headspin

What happens when you are so overwhelmed by events that your ability to think freezes up? You cannot concentrate, you become disorganized, and you lose perspective on what matters and what does not. You cannot prioritize effectively, you cannot see clearly what needs to be done, and you feel as if you can't cope. You have gone into a headspin.

What is happening here is that your high quality Bubble mode thinking cannot keep up because the frontal lobes of your brain, where it resides, are overwhelmed. This leads to impulsive judgements, impaired social interactions and emotional hijacking that leaves you angry, guilty, defensive and scared. So you become moody and look for people to blame. Yikes!

The solution is to slow down. You need to protect your frontal lobes from the over-supply of stimulation. This is a case of more haste: less speed. Instead of charging on, use the SCOPE process. Ask questions and listen. Reflect on the answers and think about what is going on slowly. If necessary; take a break. Go for a walk, make a coffee and, if you must keep working, revert to simple, routine tasks, that put little load on your cognitive functions. An ideal routine task to undertake is to tidy up your workspace. Not only is this not demanding, but it will also give you a strong sense of taking control of your environment. As we will see soon, taking control like this is a great way to combat the onset of stress symptoms.

Asking someone some questions has a second benefit: it connects you with people. Working alone boosts the chances of slipping into headspin, so reconnecting with people is a good way to shift the focus of your thinking from the problem to social interactions.

Overload Versus Overwhelm

People confuse being overwhelmed with being overloaded. Let's clarify the difference.

Overload

Overload is an objective status where you have too much work to achieve, to the required standard, with the time and resources available to you. The solution to overload lies in the Pyramid of Balance, which you saw in Chapter 1. You can either reduce the amount you take on, cut some corners, give yourself longer or secure more resources. You need to rebalance your workload by shrinking the Pyramid of Balance.

You need to prioritize ruthlessly and be prepared to say N.O. – make a Noble Objection that states, respectfully, that you must

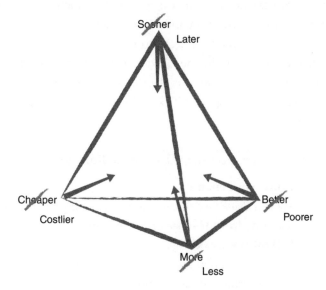

Shrinking the Pyramid of Balance

decline some calls upon your time, in order to ensure that you can deliver the things that matter most. You can learn more about the Noble Objection and how to say N.O. in my earlier book, *The Yes/No Book*.

Overwhelm

Overwhelm, on the other hand, is a wholly subjective state. It is how you feel. You can probably recall times when you had a huge mountain of work to get through – you were possibly even overloaded – but you felt in control. Yet at another time, you may have felt completely overwhelmed by a considerably lighter workload. Overwhelm tends to occur as a cumulative response to heavy workload, poor rest and diet, and other things going on in your life. Overwhelm is a stress response, in which you feel out of control.

The first thing you need to do to handle overwhelm is stop. Use the SCOPE process to avoid headspin, and ask: 'What's important?' While you are on a short break, take care of two simple physiological factors that can affect the functioning of your Bubble mode: hydration and blood sugar levels. Have a glass of water and something light to eat – fruit or nuts are ideal. When we are overwhelmed, the one thing that fails is Bubble – we cannot concentrate or make decisions. So you need a rigid routine that can displace Click and avoid you being taken over by Hum.

So instigate the seven-step Overwhelm Routine.

1. **Know your enemy**
   Make a *'Now List'* of everything on your plate that is contributing to your sense of overwhelm.
2. **Kill off the weaklings**
   Take a green pen and cross out everything that is really not important enough to bother about.

3. **Send the stragglers to the back**

   Take a blue pen and put any items that can wait 24 hours or more onto a new sheet, your *'Tomorrow List'*, and cross them off your Now List.

4. **Tackle the Tiddlers**

   Take a red pen and put a star by all the items on your Now List that will take less than five minutes – these are your *'Tiddlers'*.

5. **Frenzied attack – on your Tiddlers**

   Spend 20 minutes quickly doing as many Tiddlers as you can. Start with the first on your list and work down. Only give each one as much time as is absolutely necessary to meet the required standard.

6. **Regroup**

   With your red pen, cross off the Tiddlers you killed-off and take a break. Decide which unmarked item (your *'Big Fish'*) has top priority.

7. **Measured attack – on a Big Fish**

   Tackle your Big Fish by dividing it into steps and spend about 40 minutes on it. Only tackle steps that are urgent. Put the rest on your Tomorrow List.

At the end of this, you will have reduced your overwhelm list substantially and made decent progress on one big item. You will have spent a little over an hour, so take a proper break. Walk around, drink some water and get a nice snack. When you are ready (take at least ten to fifteen minutes), go back to step 5 and kill of some more Tiddlers, regroup and make another measured attack.

After three cycles of this, you will almost certainly have no Tiddlers, have made good progress on big tasks, and have started to feel properly in control. Few people will still feel overwhelmed at this stage. If you do, take a good long break (at least 40 minutes – ideally an hour) and get back in there.

Stress

Over the long term, overwhelm turns into the symptoms of stress. These are not pleasant: poor sleep, constant anxiety, poor health and ineffectiveness in much that you do. The stress response arises from feeling that you are not in control of what matters to you. Consequently, the way to deal with stress is to re-assert your control. Do this in four areas:

Physical: make deliberate and positive changes to the way you guard your physical wellbeing. Improve your diet, take more exercise – of any sort – and improve your rest and relaxation routines.

Mental: choose to focus on the things you *can* control. Notice the resources that you have available to you and give yourself positive messages about what you are doing, how you are coping and the progress you are making.

Environmental: look for ways you can control your environment – both your physical environment and your social environment. Tidy up and make small changes to where you work and live, and select people to socialize with who make you feel good.

Time: make clear choices about how you use your time. Prioritize carefully and say no to more things. Make time for good quality rest, exercise and socializing. Being with friends and loved ones and, in particular, laughing with them, can create a massive boost in your wellbeing.

Resilience

Resilience is a long-term ability to resist headspin, overwhelm and stress. To understand how to build resilience, we need first to recognize three psychological beliefs that trap us into states of hopelessness, where headspin and stress start to become frequent visitors.

Three Blockers to Powerhouse Effectiveness

Permanence

'It will always be like this.'

Once you get into this mind-set, it is easy to believe that the good things in your life are only the results of happy chance: problems and ineffectiveness are your default position. This is, of course, rubbish. Take the attitude that your setbacks are temporary and, with diligence, you can take control of your situation and gradually turn things around. A Powerhouse has permanent effectiveness, occasionally marred by instances of bad luck.

Pervasiveness

'The world is a bad place and I can do nothing about it.'

Once you head in this direction, anything you try will start to seem futile. But it isn't, because every change, every triumph, and everything worthwhile that mankind has built, got made one step at a time. So focus on the things you can control, deal with them to your best abilities, and look to expand the scope of your influence in the world. A Powerhouse is effective across a wide range of endeavours, with specific areas where one needs to – and can – access help and guidance.

Personalization

'It's me, it's my fault, I'm a bad/unlucky/unworthy person.'

Can you be responsible for everything that is wrong in the world, and nothing that is right? Certainly not! You are every bit as good, as lucky and as worthy as the next person. You are a Powerhouse and you are responsible for your own choices. A Powerhouse is emotionally resilient even if, sometimes, they are in the wrong place at the wrong time.

The Seven Keys to Resilience

By now, you should not be surprised to learn that you have already met all of the things you need to know about resilience. The answer lies in seven of our ten Powerhouse attitudes.

Hope

Realistic optimism is essential to a resilient mind-set. This is not like blind, glass half-full optimism, but a positive outlook and a determination to seek out beneficial opportunities. Positive emotions, like enjoyment, playfulness and affection, buffer us against hard knocks, while negative emotions decrease our ability to cope. People who spend more time smiling live longer, happier lives: I call this the Felicity Factor, after my smiling wife!

Grit

Face your fears and take them on. You can choose avoidance and deny your problems but it won't work, or you can take responsibility for your problems and find solutions.

Upright

A strong moral compass seems to enhance our resilience, and research shows that this does not need to be faith or culturally based. Wherever it comes from, acting on the urge to act ethically leaves us feeling stronger in the face of hardships.

Giving

A network of emotional support is essential in coping with the hardest of times. So to build resilience, invest in your network of friends and colleagues. Take good care of them and of your family, so that you will be able to seek their help when you need it. People with the strongest social ties and close relationships seem to cope best with traumatic life events.

Open

Another factor that correlates strongly with coping ability is mental and emotional flexibility – the ability to regulate how we think and how we express our emotions. The more choices we give ourselves and the more time we take to re-evaluate what we are doing, the better able we are to find ways out of tough situations.

Cool

Mental and physical fitness are not negotiable when it comes to resilience. Maintaining a long-term regime of good sleep, good exercise and a good diet will allow you to remain calm and resourceful under pressure, with the reserves of stamina that you need to remain disciplined and persistent.

Thankful

Recognizing all that you have to be grateful for will keep your focus on the positives and put your setbacks into perspective. And because thankfulness tends to focus on some of the most fundamental aspects of our lives, it also serves to remind us of what is most important to us. Meaning is a great motivator when we feel there is little else to drive us.

Resilience: 11 Powerhouse Pointers

1. A Powerhouse will sometimes fail. That is the price for going to the cutting edge of effectiveness. What matters is how you handle it.
2. Use the OODA Loop to take control in a fast moving situation: Observe – Orient – Decide – Act.
3. As problems build, stick with it. But don't just persevere blindly; apply Intelligent Perseverance: Perception + Judgement + Adaptability + Perseverance.

4. When shift happens, Powerhouse effectiveness means being able to deal with all the problems that arise, effectively and efficiently.

5. Suppress your Hum and engage Bubble with the SCOPE Process: Stop, Clarify, Options, Proceed, Evaluate.

6. In times of shift, choose your Powerhouse mode from: leader, exploration, process, fix-it, crisis and supporting modes.

7. Overload is an objective state of having more to do than you can possibly accomplish. Rebalance your workload by shrinking the Pyramid of Balance.

8. Overwhelm is a stress response, in which you feel out of control: instigate the overwhelm routine to regain a sense of control.

9. Control stress by taking control of your physical and mental states, your environment and how you use your time.

10. Avoid the three mind-sets of permanence, pervasiveness and personalization, which block Powerhouse effectiveness

11. 'Weebles wobble ... but they don't fall down' – build your resilience, with the seven keys to long-term resilience: hope, grit, upright, giving, open, cool and thankful.

9
Growth
Know When and Where to Stop

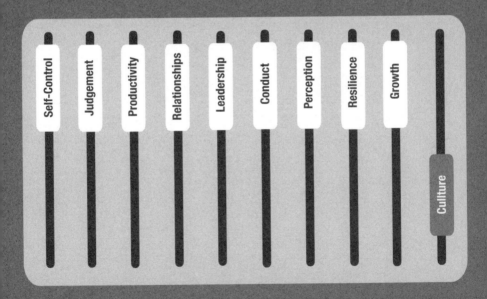

You effectively achieved what you set out to achieve – you delivered the goods. Another great result for the *Powerhouse*: congratulations! Now it is time to wrap it up and move on. You need to know when and how to stop but, more important still, you need to learn from what you have achieved, to harness the value of your success by growing and evolving as a professional.

When to Stop

**At the time of starting, the time to stop is
defined by what success will look like.**

A Powerhouse knows when to stop ... When it is no longer
effective to continue. When the job is done.

At the time of starting out on your compelling cause, the time to
stop is defined by what success will look like. You must define
'Done'. Define Done in terms of your outcome and the specifi-
cations, functions and behaviours that go with it.

When You Reach Done, You Must Stop

When you reach Done, you must stop. Consider the alternative for a moment. What would happen if, instead, you put in
continued effort to further and further improve the polish on
your work? When you do this, you will be subject to the law
of diminishing returns: a lot of extra work leads to little extra
benefit. This is not effective: it is the Pareto curve we met in
Chapter 1. Let's look at it again.

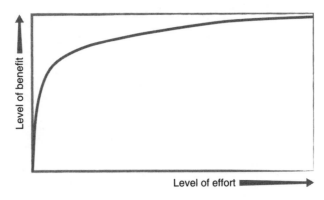

The law of diminishing returns

The consequence of not finishing, when finishing is the right thing to do, is that you will never be able to move on, fully embrace the next compelling cause that matters, and will not be able to fully reflect on what you have learned.

The Powerhouse alternative is to finish; to stop and evaluate what you have achieved. Don't ask: *'How can I make it better?'* Instead, ask: *'What is the next opportunity?'*

If the next opportunity comes from a development of what you have just created – or from an incremental improvement – then that will become your next compelling cause, so define what the new Done will look like and start planning.

The Cycle of Improvement

This leads to a cycle of improvements, with each one contributing real additional value by extending the opportunities it addresses.

If you think about the activity levels of the cycle of improvement, you might picture a series of waves of activity, with checkpoints along the way. These are the checkpoints we met in the Geometry of Change, in Chapter 2. Now you can recognize the Outcome Check as really asking 'is it Done?' If it is, at the

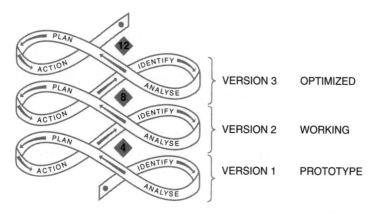

The cycle of improvement

next iteration of the identify stage you will look for new opportunities that would arise if you work further on the project. You are looking at where you are on the Pareto curve.

How to Stop

Finish what you are doing in an orderly manner.

You have achieved what you set out to achieve – you delivered the goods: congratulations! Now finish it in an orderly manner.

This means four things:

1. Wrapping up the details.
2. Learning the lessons.
3. Saying thank you to everyone who helped.
4. Moving on.

Wrapping Up the Details

Whatever your outcome, there may well be some loose ends to tie up before you can move on. If you do not deal with these, you will find that these small but necessary uncompleted steps will hang over you, draining you of some of your mental energy. Unfortunately, these will often take the form of simple, dull, administrative tasks that will hardly pose a challenge for a Powerhouse like you. But being a Powerhouse is about effectiveness and the diligence and perseverance to get on with what needs to be done. So grit your teeth and do it.

Apply the principles of 5S that we saw in Chapter 3 to sort, systematize and sweep up after yourself, so everything is standardized and sustainable, allowing you to move on with confidence.

Learning the Lessons

An essential part of a Powerhouse culture is constant learning and growth. This is what it means to be open.

It is easy to save the lessons for the end of what you are working on. If, however, you are working on a long project, then create review points for yourself. All of the evidence suggests that taking time out to reflect on what you have done and how it has worked is the route to greater understanding, maturity and even wisdom.

We hear a lot about the importance of learning from our mistakes; which is vital. This is the 'win or learn' mind-set, which is critical to a Powerhouse because you will go to the edge and therefore sometimes fall.

Win or Learn

When you get something wrong, or if excellence evades you, what matters is how you handle it. Admit it, figure out the causes, and put in place ways to prevent a repeat. A Powerhouse works towards constant success.

Win and Learn

Too often, we win and do not learn. We assume our success was somehow inevitable and don't stop to figure out what it was that helped bring it about. As important as the 'win or learn' mind-set is the 'win and learn' mind-set.

By applying your curiosity to why you succeeded and what choices contributed to your success, you will be focusing on the positives that not only will help you succeed in the future, but will also help build resilience, as we saw in the last chapter. And we tend to get more of what we pay attention to. So ask:

- What were your principal triumphs?
- How did you achieve them?
- What ideas, contributions or events made the most difference?
- What were the most surprising events and outcomes?
- What would be your priorities on day one of a similar initiative?

Where people have helped you, help them to reflect in the same way, and give them your assessment of how they contributed. It is important to recognize what people have put into their work.

Do and Learn

You don't have to have a success to learn. Everything a Powerhouse does is an opportunity for reflection and learning. That is the nature of experimentation after all. You should be looking for opportunities to try new ways to do things and explore alternative methods. And once you learn something new, take it out for a spin and practice it, to embed your learning and enhance it by noticing the subtleties you overlooked at the start.

Can't Do and Learn

What if you can't do something? Will you get frustrated and give up? Of course not: to a Powerhouse, this is the ideal opportunity to grow your abilities. Try and figure it out, research it, watch someone else do it, or ask for help. As you would expect, the Powerhouse Loop applies nicely to the process of learning new skills.

- **Identify**: determine what you need to learn.
- **Analyse**: Review what you know already, what you need to learn, and then access new knowledge to fill the gap.
- **Plan**: decide how you will break the skill down into manageable chunks.
- **Action**: practice the most important skills first and build up your level of competence, so you can ...
- Return to the identify step.

Can't Stop Learning

A Powerhouse will not stand still, you will not rest on your laurels, you will never stop learning. Continuous evolution and growth as a professional is a mark of a Powerhouse attitude. And that attitude has one thing at its heart: curiosity. Take an interest in everything, seek feedback from every source and invest in learning from anywhere you can: books, articles, seminars and colleagues.

Saying Thank You to Everyone Who Helped

Recognition is important and so is some form of thanks. Nothing says thank you like celebrating success. When we celebrate our successes, we become more aware of what we have achieved, which makes us feel more confident. Next time, this confidence can help boost our performance, so that we get better results and therefore more success. Celebration is therefore at the heart of a virtuous cycle of performance improvement and success.

Bring together the learning and celebration with stories. People love to hear and read success stories ... but not as much as personal stories. Tell the story of the people involved. Use whatever media are appropriate to publicize their success and how they achieved it: house magazines, websites and social media can all create a buzz around your project or initiative. And a Powerhouse does not need to brag about your own success when you can tell the stories of the people you led, and gain reflected glory from their achievements.

Moving on
So, what next?

A Powerhouse is always thinking towards future opportunities, so you will want to update you résumé and think about the next set of skills and experience you want to acquire. There is a great debate about the relative benefits of focusing on a narrow specialism, for which you will become well known and sought after, or aiming for breadth of experience. A Powerhouse knows the value of balance: if you are an expert at nothing, then you have little that will distinguish you from your peers. But, if your expertise is too narrow, you will neither see, nor be able to exploit, the full range of opportunities that are available. Develop a breadth of knowledge and experience, but take opportunities to deepen your skills in areas that excite you. Ideally look out for capabilities that are rare, yet which seem to be in demand. These are the ones that offer big opportunities now.

One day, you will look at your career as a succession of projects and initiatives. Together, they will form the portfolio that will either make you proud of what you achieved or sorry about the opportunities you missed. What is the next opportunity?

Whatever you do next, always look for ways to associate with success: to work with people who take pride in what they do, who are positive and accept setbacks as a chance to learn, and who are Powerhouse performers.

Chapter 10 is a bonus chapter. In it, we will look at how you can create a Powerhouse organization. Maybe your 'what next' will be to take some of what you have learned and embed it into your organization's culture?

Growth: 6 Powerhouse Pointers

1. At the time of starting, the time to stop is defined by what success will look like.
2. When you reach Done, you must stop.
3. Finish what you are doing in an orderly manner.
4. An essential part of a Powerhouse culture is constant learning and growth.
5. Curiosity: A Powerhouse cannot stop learning.
6. A Powerhouse is always thinking towards future opportunities.

10
Culture
Create a Powerhouse Organization

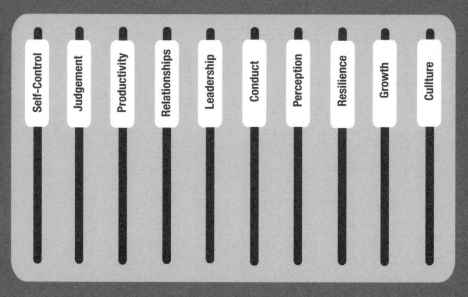

Self-Control | Judgement | Productivity | Relationships | Leadership | Conduct | Perception | Resilience | Growth | Culture

An organization full of *Powerhouse* performers: is it possible? What would it feel like if everyone, from your top team down, adopted the Powerhouse principles?

If you want this, you have to start from a simple assumption: that this is what people really want. They want to do the right thing, they want to be effective, and they want to make a difference.

By now, I hope that you feel you have all of the tools and resources to turn yourself into a real Powerhouse. But is this enough?

A Powerhouse is a restless spirit and you may just be wondering: 'How can I bring my Powerhouse attitudes to my organization? What would it take to build a Powerhouse Culture, where everyone could be like this?'

Powerhouse Culture

A Powerhouse culture is one of openness, collaboration and genuine empowerment.

We can extend the psychology of success, which we discovered in Chapter 5, to create a thriving Powerhouse organization. It creates a culture of openness, collaboration and genuine empowerment.

Empowerment is a much-used term in modern management and it is rarer than many organizations would like to believe. It means a deep self-confidence coupled with true authority to make decisions and act. It is a result of the right cultural values and practices. There are seven principles of a Powerhouse culture.

Principle 1: Sort Out the Rules

Organizations are often full of out-of-date practices and even rules that get in the way of people doing their jobs – let alone doing them as effectively as a Powerhouse. 'Why is this organization so stupid?' we hear people say; especially shortly after they join. But after a while, we start to hear: 'Well, it's just the way things are, I guess' instead. We shouldn't have to put up with this.

Give people the resources and the structures that they need to help them work effectively. Get rid of out-of-date rules that no longer serve the organization or its people. This is about distinguishing between treating people well, and treating them according to the rules. If someone breaks a rule, before criticizing or reprimanding them, first check that it is not a stupid rule whose purpose no longer exists. Ideally, a Powerhouse organization will replace rules entirely with valuable customs and deeply held values. This way, people will act according to an implicit rule-set, which they impose upon themselves and therefore accept willingly. Expect your most senior people to role model the behaviours and values that you want to see in your people.

Your organization should make available all the resources that your people need – and make them easier to access and give your people more authority to command them. We worry about people wasting this, or pilfering that, but ignore the fact that many of them hold the reputation and future of our organizations in their hands, from the salesperson who holds a valuable client relationship, to the maintenance engineer who keeps the machinery operating … and safe.

Also, make information easy to access. Create mechanisms for data sharing that discourage private pools of data. When everyone has wholly independent access to the widest data set, interpretations will vary and the quality of discussions and decision-making will improve. Encourage people to come together to share what everyone else does. In the emerging era of big data, there is no excuse for not looking at how to make better use of information.

Encourage an orderly and tidy 5S culture: sort, systematize, sweep, standardize and sustain (see Chapter 3 for more details). Don't do it to create another set of rules, but to make people's lives easier, more predictable and more pleasant.

Finally, prioritize good quality decision-making over adherence to the rules. Train people in decision processes and how to avoid bias, and then systematically give them the tools and information that they need, to practice highly effective 4P (Proof + Process + Perspective + Protection) decision-making (see Chapter 2) and robust planning (Chapter 3).

Principle 2: Supercharge Commitment

Workplaces are primarily social in nature and we forget this at our peril. Most people working full time will spend more of their waking hours with their work colleagues than with the person they have chosen as their life partner. Embed within your systems and processes ways to be considerate towards people, and encourage everyone to be nice to everyone with whom they come into contact. In environments like this, people will flourish.

The impact of positive and negative comments is astonishing. People and whole organizations flourish when subjected to a positive atmosphere, whilst constant negativity and criticism will grind down even the most resilient person. Work towards a ratio of positive to negative comments within meetings, conversations and discussions of three to one or better.

Linked to this is the value of encouraging a focus on people's strengths, giving everyone the chance to grow and master their work, and the autonomy to make their own choices. Allocate work in ways that recognize people's preferences and make the best use of their strengths. Ensure that people understand the meaning and purpose behind everything you ask them to do, to ensure that they do not become demotivated simply because they don't know the reason why they need to do it.

Prepare people properly for new roles and tasks. This does not necessarily mean that they have to have 100 per cent of the skills and experience that they will need, but that there are support and safety mechanisms in place that recognize the gap and allow them to learn with confidence. Better still, identify talent early, and create opportunities for them to learn the skills they will need if they wish to progress.

Finally, provide a range of amenities that allow your people to manage their stress levels and remain healthy and resilient. Even something as simple (and inexpensive) as providing fresh fruit, healthy snacks and a quiet room to think and reflect can make a huge difference. If you can do other things that support healthy social lives and active exercise, then so much the better. Be as flexible as you can be over working hours and ensure that work stations are provided with the most ergonomically effective furniture and equipment.

Principle 3: Strengthen Performance

People want to feel a pride in what they do, and a sense of improving their skills. Give them the means and encouragement to do their best and to improve their practice. And when they do so: celebrate their successes with them.

Help people to learn in the ways that suit them by providing a range of learning and development opportunities. Some people love the 'standard' training room experience: others don't. Avoid a faddish jump into new forms of learning though. It is best to create a balanced portfolio of learning alternatives.

Why is it that when many people my age were at school, we were told to work on our own? Anything else was seen as cheating. We know better now, so encourage collaboration and provide the tools that will make it effective in your environment. Also encourage the development of Positive Energy Networks (Chapter 4) so that people feel part of highly charged and creative groupings. Consider allowing these groupings time to work on their own projects.

Reward, remunerate and promote on merit. Don't just look at material success: also look for the people who act as great role models for the Powerhouse qualities and attitudes you want to encourage, like positivity, cooperation and grit.

Finally, in giving feedback, adopt a bias towards positive, diamond feedback (Chapter 5). Make it frequent, immediate and helpful. When people do well, celebrate their performance.

Principle 4: Prioritize Investment for Strategic Opportunity

No organization has infinite capacity, resources and time. Yours will therefore be constrained in the initiatives that it can undertake, and stretching itself too far will mean that some will inevitably fail ... and they won't always be the least important.

Choosing your organization's activities wisely requires the board or senior management to define a few vital priorities – Powerhouse priorities – for each year and each quarter. These will occupy the majority of time for the management team at all levels. They should be spread among: winning today – exploiting current opportunities; winning tomorrow – gearing up for forthcoming changes; and winning in the future – exploring the directions for the future.

First, you must understand the nature of your organization's business, as a basis for creative thinking and informed decision-making. Three things to understand are:

1. *Your organization's destination*
   What is your competitive goal, what are the products and services you aim to offer, and what vision, or intention, drives your organization forward?
2. *Your customers and clients*
   Which customers or clients offer you the best opportunity to reach your destination?
3. *Your products and services*
   What products and services offer your organization the best opportunity to serve the customers and clients you have chosen?

Then you must analyse your opportunities, to find a strategy that offers a long-term view of the choices you will make and the risks you will take. It allows you to do things that may not make sense in terms of winning now, or even tomorrow, because they are designed to help you win in the future. A strategy is the overall direction of your organization's travel, and it recognizes that you will need to fill in the details – the tactics – as you get closer to events.

Having understood your business, you need to analyse three things:

1. *Your potential sources of competitive advantage*
   Lower costs, reduced prices, a different offering to that of your competitors, specialization in a narrow niche or exceptional loyalty from a well-defined customer base?
2. *The assets you have to create this competitive advantage*
   Products and services, your reputation, your plant, equipment and property, your organization's abilities, knowledge and expertise, and its processes, systems and intellectual property?

3. *What are the opportunities to seize competitive advantage, and serve your customers and clients?*
    Put together the work you have done to identify your opportunities. Now you need to think about which of them will be the most productive in creating value.

Your organization must be productive in creating value for its stakeholders, and the tool we will use is portfolio prioritization.

If your organization is going to adopt a few priorities for the coming year that will occupy the majority of its time, they need to be the right ones; the ones that have the greatest potential to create value for your organization's stakeholders. These are not problems to solve, but opportunities, so evaluate each option based on the level of benefit and the likelihood of success, or feasibility.

The following diagram illustrates how to do this, by rating each opportunity on two simple scales of benefit and feasibility.

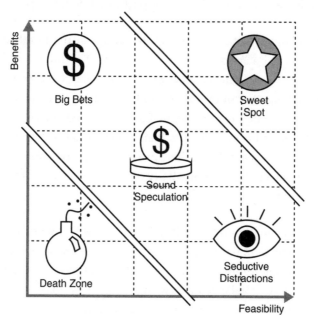

Prioritizing a Powerhouse portfolio

We measure benefit in terms of the value of potential savings or income, on the perceptions of value among your most important stakeholders (maybe customers, shareholders or staff), and on the extent to which this opportunity is consistent with the long-term direction in which you want to move your organization.

We measure feasibility by considering things like risk, complexity, level of investment needed, timescale and number of external constraints or inter-relationships that would need to be managed.

Between the diagonal tramlines are the opportunities that offer proportionate risk and reward. Most of your opportunities will lie in this zone because, more often than not, you get what you pay for. Be suspicious of opportunities that appear to occupy the Sweet Spot of high benefit and high feasibility. Test your assumptions particularly hard, because if they prove to be robust, then these are the first opportunities to take up.

On the other hand, dismiss opportunities in the Death Zone. These will be hard to make work and offer little benefit in return for your efforts. Also be cautious about the Seductive Distractions that offer little benefit, even though they are easy to achieve. Put a few into your Powerhouse portfolio to generate quick and easy successes that you can celebrate and use to motivate the team. But if there are too many, you fritter a lot of energy on a basket of potentially disconnected small initiatives with little cumulative value.

Choose a small number of Big Bets, for which you will need to invest substantial time, effort and risk. These are often the truly transformative opportunities, but the level of risk suggests it can be wise to balance them with a range of Solid Speculations that carry greater chances of significant, though not astounding, success.

Keep in mind that both axes offer uncertainty; so do not try to be too precise. Five point scales: very low, low, medium, high and very high will suffice. Consider the implications for your choice of occupying one place lower on each axis and simply ask: how would that affect your decisions?

Principle 5: Use Time as the Strategic Asset it is

It is time to recognize that people are not your most valuable asset: time is. You can replace people – when time is gone, you can never replace it. People have limited time, so why aren't you budgeting it carefully?

Doing the wrong thing has a cost to your organization: the opportunity cost. This is the additional value that you forego by not pursuing the better opportunity.

It is time to stop doing the work that comes across our desks and work backwards from the organization's priorities. People will feel more effective and will be more effective when they trust that the organization will support them when they make strategic choices in which compelling causes to pursue and what to say no to. They need to know that their priorities are their organization's priorities. So your organization must help people to be more effective in their choices.

Empower people to make good choices about their work, by showing them what opportunities meet the organization's purpose and offer the best combination of value and risk. Within this loose framework of priorities and causes, managers have the freedom to make their own choices. This is like the military principle of 'commander's intent': spelling out the objectives and letting people interpret it in the light of real conditions.

You know that shift happens, so do not freeze a set of outcomes into an institutional rule-set. Introduce a quarterly review of strategic time management priorities, using tools like horizon scanning to identify changes in your organization's external and internal environment, and then analyse the impact they will have.

Effectiveness = Focus + Adaptability

Principle 6: Sanction N.O.

Time is a strategic asset, so people must focus their endeavour on the organization's priorities. To do so, they must be able to make choices about how they use their time, and therefore to say 'no' to less strategic or valuable requests. You must support them in this.

Principle 5 showed you how to be clear about what the organization's priorities are, and what decision criteria people should use in assessing how to use their time. Use them to encourage your people to exercise Powerhouse focus on what matters most.

Allow people to make their own evaluation of how to meet those priorities. There will always be more things that your best people could do than the time available to do them. Doing everything is not their job (or yours). Their job is to use the time they have to deliver the greatest value to your organization and its primary stakeholders. So help them to see through the fog of alternatives and to evaluate their choices against the right values. When you get your top-level purpose right and communicate it well, people will make better decisions.

Consequently, you must allow people to say N.O. to opportunities and requests that are not as valuable as the alternatives. And you must back them up fully when they say no for the right reasons – even if they made an interpretational mistake and got their decision wrong. N.O. – a Noble Objection – is a principle that will deliver real focus.

Principle 7: Sharpen Up Your Organization

Learn from your mistakes. But, more importantly, learn from your successes. Every experience is a valuable source of inspiration and insight, as long as people make the time to reflect on what has happened and to inquire into the reasons. Evaluate the conditions and behaviours that create excellence and find ways to repeat, enhance and embed them.

Create processes and habits that encourage reflective learning, both individually and among teams of colleagues (Chapter 9).

When you facilitate the process of reflection, focus on asking questions that reveal what is best about your organization, your people and your practices. This appreciative approach, highlighting the positive, will engender a culture of positivity where people are more courageous and better motivated.

Learning is not enough: you need to use that learning to build change. Create compelling causes to repeat, enhance and embed what you learn into procedures that work or new, improved, practices.

Make the Powerhouse Loop (Chapter 1) a fundamental driver for your organization's business cycle and for constant improvement in how you serve your customers and clients.

Culture: 7 Powerhouse Pointers

1. Sort out the rules: make it easy for everyone to become a Powerhouse.
2. Supercharge commitment: build a positive environment where people can use and develop their strengths.

3. Strengthen performance: encourage people to perform at their best, and recognize it appropriately.
4. Prioritize investment for strategic opportunity: balance winning today, winning tomorrow and winning in the future.
5. Use time as the strategic asset it is: focus everyone on strategic outcomes and empower them to make decisions accordingly.
6. Sanction N.O.: Noble Objections allow people to decline work where they could use their time for more effective effort.
7. Sharpen up your organization: always be learning ... and implementing what you learn.

And if You Can Do All of This ...

'Seven principles' does not sound a lot. But they are seven big steps for many organizations. There is more you could do too, but the overwhelming secret for Powerhouse success is this:

'Focus on what matters most, do it really well, do it relentlessly, and constantly scan the horizon for the next shift. Follow the Powerhouse Loop, and you will succeed.'

Good Luck

Mike

ABOUT THE AUTHOR

Many people have described Mike Clayton as a Powerhouse.

In five years, he has written 12 books, whilst extending his speaking and seminar business. These five years have also been happy and busy years at home, as his writing career started a week after the birth of his daughter, and a month or so after moving to a new home in a new town with his new wife.

Mike has always tried to be effective in everything he does, and learned his business, management and professional skills as a management consultant, leading large engagements on behalf of the international consulting firm, Deloitte. Having established two training businesses after leaving Deloitte, Mike now focuses his work on writing, on business, management and personal effectiveness seminars, and as a platform speaker.

All of Mike's books, seminars and training programmes are about being effective as a professional, manager or leader, but Powerhouse is the first to bring the theme of effectiveness right to the fore, and so marks an important milestone in Mike's professional career.

Mike lives in Hampshire, England, with his wife and daughter.

ALSO BY MIKE CLAYTON

Mike Clayton is author of 12 other books to date.

The Influence Agenda
A Systematic Approach to Aligning Stakeholders in Times of Change
Palgrave Macmillan, 2014

How to Manage a Great Project
On Budget, On Target, On Time
Pearson, 2014

How to Speak so People Listen
Grab attention, hold it, and get your message across
Pearson, 2013

The Yes / No Book
How to Do Less… and Achieve More
Pearson, 2012

Smart to Wise
The Seven Pillars for True Success
Marshall Cavendish, 2012

Brilliant Project Leader
What the best project leaders know, do and say to get results, every time
Pearson, 2012

Brilliant Stress Management
How to manage stress in any situation
Pearson, 2011

Risk Happens!
Managing risk and avoiding failure in business projects
Marshall Cavendish, 2011

Brilliant Time Management
What the most productive people know, do and say
Pearson, 2011

Brilliant Influence
What the most influential people know, do and say
Pearson, 2011

The Handling Resistance Pocketbook
Management Pocketbooks, 2010

The Management Models Pocketbook
Management Pocketbooks, 2009

BOOK MIKE CLAYTON

Mike is a conference speaker and business consultant. He speaks at conferences, team events, workshops and seminars for companies, associations, public authorities and not-for-profit organizations.

Mike's topics are all around the subject or personal and professional effectiveness. As well as his new Powerhouse seminar and keynote, he can develop bespoke programmes for your organization.

His other seminar and speaking topics include advanced communication, management and leadership, wisdom, and project management and the management of change.

If you want to spread Powerhouse effectiveness within your organization, Mike is available for speaking engagements, seminars and training and, with the publisher, can offer special deals on bulk purchases of this book.

You can book Mike to talk about Powerhouse or another topic at:

www.mikeclayton.co.uk

or

www.beapowerhouse.co.uk

WHO ELSE NEEDS POWERHOUSE?

A Powerhouse does not work alone. And you will be even more effective surrounded by other Powerhouse performers. Who do you know that wants to be more effective and to achieve a greater impact?

Why not do them a favour? Call, email or tweet them today about *Powerhouse*. Better still: send them a copy. Who knows; it may just transform the way they work. What better way can there be to strengthen your relationship in under a minute?

Contact Mike or the publishers, Capstone, to enquire about orders of *Powerhouse*, for your whole team.

mike@mikeclayton.co.uk

INDEX

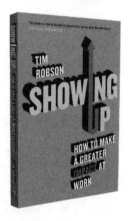

get more

Your monthly dose of business brilliance - articles, interviews, videos and more

Sign up to our newsletter today!